Speaking of the Middle Ages

Parlez du moyen âge

Translated by
Sarah White

Foreword by
Eugene Vance

Speaking of the Middle Ages

by Paul Zumthor

University of Nebraska Press
Lincoln & London

The paper in this book meets
the guidelines for
permanence and durability
of the Committee on
Production Guidelines for
Book Longevity of the
Council on Library Resources.

Publication of this book was
aided by a grant from The
Andrew W. Mellon Foundation.

Library of Congress
Cataloging-in-Publication Data
Zumthor, Paul, 1915-
Speaking of the Middle Ages =
Parler du Moyen Age.
(Regents studies
in medieval culture)
Bibliography: p.
1. Literature, Medieval –
History and criticism – Theory,
etc.   I. Title.   II. Title: Parler
du Moyen Age.   III. Series.
PN673.Z8313   1986
809'.02   85-16545
ISBN 0-8032-4907-1
(alkaline paper)

To Jean Massin

Contents

Eugene Vance

Foreword

For all its brevity, this book by Paul Zumthor traces the major turning points in a long and still vigorous career. But it can also serve as a guide for the perplexed medievalist who may have perceived certain impasses in the methods of orthodox medievalism (or what Zumthor playfully calls *le médiévisme de papa*), yet who does not know how to seek alternatives for future criticism and research.

By virtue of his early collaboration with the great master of philology, Walther von Wartburg (among others), Paul Zumthor is surely one of the best-trained philologists of our time. Yet, already with his first publications he began to move beyond that heritage. Moreover, the spirit of open-ended quest that marks all Zumthor's major writings endures in this short book, despite its occasional (but unserious) crepuscular tone. This is the unpolemical and generous search of a mind seeking not its own monumentality, but new paradigms of understanding. These are necessary to account for a radically new experience of an epoch that has been, on the one hand, grievously sequestered from modern critical thought by medievalists themselves and, on the other, ignored by antihistorical linguists and theoreticians of the 1960s and '70s who have staunchly declined to investigate the rich medieval underpinnings of their own thought.

Although Zumthor's work has been widely translated into other languages, and although he has resided in North America for the past dozen years, this book (first published in France in 1980) is his first to appear in English. Moreover, it appears at a time when the teaching of French medieval literature (and perhaps that of other Romance languages as well) has reached an all-time low in the United States, at least in the present century. One shudders to speculate how many graduates of distinguished American institutions have become teachers of French without having ever dealt seriously with a single medieval text.

This book will surely not dictate the future of French medievalism, but it will, I hope, fuel the search for new perspectives. That is the goal, moreover, of the series in which this book is now published.

A striking feature of this book is its array of allusions to non-French and nonmedievalist critics who have informed Paul Zumthor's intellectual disposition. As we might expect, Zumthor confronts problems that are hardly confined to French medievalism as a discipline, for instance, the problem of authorial subjectivity (which still beleaguers Anglo-American medievalism), or of grasping and expressing the historical presuppositions both of a medieval text *and* of its modern interpretation. As the emphasis on "pure" theory wanes, the dream of returning to "pure" history is now clearly seen either as a self-delusion of the modern critic or else as an ideological ruse. But how do we grasp the inherent critical consciousness of a given medieval text, and how do we integrate into our own critical discourse the multiple determinations of history that relate us to that text? In his ongoing dialogue with modern German hermeneuticians, Zumthor grapples creatively with this question. Critics of literatures other than that of medieval France will surely gain from Zumthor's speculations about many other problems as well, problems which, simply because they have begun to be addressed seriously by medievalists, have suddenly made the field of medieval studies one of the most dynamic of the modern curriculum.

Sarah White

Translator's Preface

This translation was prepared in consultation with Professor Zumthor, whom I wish to thank for painstaking advice, and for understanding in the face of inevitable losses. Further thanks are due to Eugene Vance, a sensitive and thorough editor. In the preparation of the manuscript, I had financial help from Franklin and Marshall College, and word processing help from Lee Henry and Vera Gmuca. None of the above, of course, are responsible for infelicities in the present text.

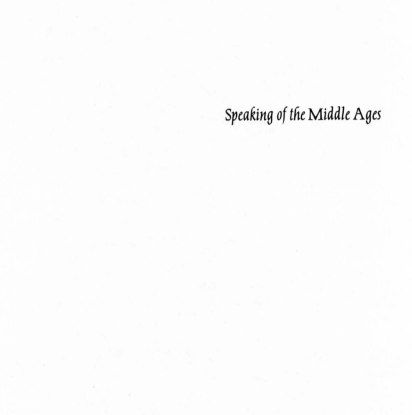

Speaking of the Middle Ages

§·

Justifications

Several works published over the last ten years, notably in France and Germany, have revived a venerable debate that places history "on trial," a trial that has lasted since the time of Thucydides. But now the business seems serious, because it questions, radically at times, not only the methods and the usefulness of a science, but also the very nature of that science and the epistemological premises underlying its practice. I would like this book to be read in the same light as those studies. Indeed, it may make a contribution to the discussion—limited, to be sure, but useful because it is specific.

Of course, in leafing through these pages, my reader may be surprised to find that I speak almost exclusively of medieval studies, especially of that branch called "literary" (a particularly inadequate term). I must therefore offer some preliminary explanations. Along the way, I will not apologize for speaking in the first person. This is not a stylistic device, but an intellectual necessity. After thirty-five years of a career that slowly draws to a close, false modesty is meaningless before the final void to which my uncertain quest has led me—the quest for an intensity, for some sudden emotion that might prove worthwhile, an enterprise involving the whole being. For quite a long time now the landscape in which I thought I could wander at will has seemed to be shrinking. However, its dimensions have been not so much reduced as concentrated. We no longer move in a universe with vast outspread dimensions but toward the improbable point from which, for an instant, we may glimpse the line of flight.

3

What remains to be said? Only this: from this zone of extreme poverty to which we have come wearing our critic's garb, the territory traversed in middle life begins to take on relief and fresh color as we turn and look back. For a long time, we walked there with our eyes half closed. That, at least, is what we tell ourselves; now that we will not retravel the route, we can better see which way it led us, among what pitfalls and what green pastures. And if a bit of the landscape remains to be traversed, we will walk it from now on without undue illusion or undue fatigue, having become, willing or not, a part of history.

It is not a question of speaking about oneself, still less of retreating into a den of memories. It is a matter of choosing, prudently (for time is precious and urges us on), the most directly accessible reference point. Others are free to illustrate a half century of scholarly or social achievement by tracing the biography of a mentor or colleague. But why take that course, when what counts in the end is neither he nor I? What counts is the possibility of identifying in an emblematic way the social function fulfilled by that individual (that is, by his work) as part of a given project, a given task, a given field of thought or research to which events (for want of a natural inclination) attached him for a fairly long time. In this way, the project, the task, or the field may be considered through the mediation of a person, that is, otherwise than in the library.

In my case, events converged with a natural inclination (awakened in a distant time while I was studying the history of law) to propel me quite early toward the dubious status of medievalist. In fact, since 1942 or '43, I have not ceased to be interested in medieval civilization, especially in its linguistic substructures and poetic manifestations. That is the domain in which, almost without interruption, I have taught and pursued my modest course of research. I have had fun doing it; I have also known hours of deep pleasure. These circumstances concern only me, and I attach no general value to them. Nonetheless, they have allowed me, little by little, a slow and delightful experience whose effect, on the level of imagery and ideas, was so marked that I would be untruthful not to acknowledge it now in whatever I say: from the place that was mine by choice and by profession, windows looked out in all possible directions; one gesture sufficed to open the shutters; all things were offered to this appetite for seeing, for experiencing—and, if possible, for understanding.

But I was not alone in this. The compartmentalization of disciplines imposed by our mentors' practice did not always prevent intrusions. In the fifties, for example, a dynamic relation began to link our own limited activity with the domain of the human sciences.[1] This relation presented an analogy with the one which attached us personally, as twentieth-century scholars, to our own teaching and research activity. The object of this activity, medieval texts, constituted an aggregate that touched on several others: the texts as such, the facts of medieval culture, historical facts in general. Any modification, brought about by a discovery, an analytic refinement, or a methodological innovation, in one of these aggregates, had repercussions on all the others. Therefore, the day-to-day problems arising in medieval studies were more or less common to a large number of specialized disciplines; perhaps they were even universal. Just as the object of our study was becoming part of that organic whole formed by the traces of human memory, our discourse was called upon, as if by vocation, to become part of that very memory.

Of course, one had to want to open the windows fairly wide, to create a draft, a movement of perceptions and concepts that would permit an incessant coming and going between here and elsewhere, between the past and the lived present, if not the glimpsed future. Such a movement would allow us to overcome, without abolishing, the past as history, and further, perhaps, to emerge from our ethnocentric ghetto and tear ourselves away from comfortable anachronisms. This was a fragile intention, doomed to dissolve in verbiage unless it could be consolidated by extensive, precise information. The information would, of course, be heterogeneous. One would have to choose one's own fraction of it: internal and external, some of it first-hand, some of it borrowed, with light shed on some more distant fields, so that each person's specialty would function as a central flame from which other zones would extend concentrically, and warmth with decreasing intensity would emanate at once from this source, and from others farther away.

Many (though not most) of those with whom I came to associate in the course of the years shared this conception of our task. We did not like the thought that a European medievalist might be without a notion of the sumptuous Asia of the eighth, tenth, and twelfth centuries, or of the empires of West Africa. Total ignorance or, worse, indifference to these things seemed to us suspect, even intolerable, when accompanied by complacency. It hardly mattered that what little we knew of these other areas had no great effect on our actual practice; at the level of intellectual prejudice, at least, we were loosening bonds.

In one area close to ours, it seemed inconceivable that a specialist in French "medieval literature" should not be at ease with that inseparable body of "literatures" that come down to us from the same period in Latin and other Romance (if not all European) languages. But this was not the only perspective to emerge: a second one took in the history of economic developments, of social movements, of mentalities, of customs, even of climates. A third (in fact, a privileged one among many medievalists for about a decade) was the complex of speculations and discourses engendered, since the early fifties, by an inquiry into "the literary fact," a complex we might more or less subsume under the title "phenomenology of the text."

Of course, not one of us cherished the ambition to do original work in all these areas at once. The time of *Summas* is past. A work of even remotely encyclopedic design requires collaboration, often of numerous teams. Nevertheless, it is all the more necessary to keep the windows open, unless we want to die of suffocation, that is, of lassitude and disinterest; perhaps I should add: unless we want to renounce all hope even of seeing the facts, much less of interpreting them.

It was with this conviction that a few of us in my generation, all over Europe, began to reform our ways of working and our habits of thinking and feeling. For my part, I attempted from that time on, with varying success, to place myself at some vantage point from which medieval texts might raise questions that applied to any text, if only by illustrating differences.

So the reader will understand, I think, why and how, in the

following pages, references I make to medieval studies involve a somewhat intentional ambiguity. My remarks concern a broad spectrum of the human sciences, but do so only through a particular discipline I know well, one whose limitations I will not be so foolish as to ignore.

§§.

An Overview

For several years now, despite a certain pessimism in universities, many signs have appeared that proclaim a renewal of medieval studies, affecting both their procedures and the interest they arouse.

We must distinguish two aspects of this renewal: one concerns the researchers' basic approach; the other, the curious but uninitiated public. A series of lectures and round tables organized at the Pompidou Center in January, 1979, was entitled "The Modernity of the Middle Ages." This expression, like all titles, is something of a paradox or else an outright slogan. But the phrase is capable of taking on meaning. It would be easy to enumerate the evidence for that possibility, discernible in comic strips as well as in films and television on both sides of the Atlantic. I could mention Cassenti's *Roland*, Bresson's *Lancelot*, Eric Rohmer's fine *Perceval*, the two "Grails" (fiction and theater) by Jacques Roubaud and Florence Delay. But, in the end, I wonder about the "modernity" of these works. Modern, why? How? In the void at the crossroads of the ideological and the imaginary lay the whole field of the possible, to repeat the terms in which Daniel Poirion presented these 1979 programs. Let the distortions of commercialism appropriate this inquiry and threaten to stifle it with noise; that is not what primarily concerns me. We will turn the matter around by speaking of the *otherness* of the "Middle Ages" (or let's say, in Fernand Braudel's phrase, that cultural era in which we seek our object), this "Middle Ages" which in other respects is truly "modern."[2]

At times, what literate people expect of the medievalist is not a daring philosophical exhortation (in the style current around 1830) but a discourse on humanity. At other times, they demand an insight into the origins, manifestations, and ultimate ends of culture. Whatever perspective such people may adopt, they implicitly acknowledge a difference between their own time and the Middle Ages. Perhaps their curiosity is based in part on a vague desire to escape the oppressiveness of the civilization they have created: in that case their "Middle Ages" takes on more or less the same qualities as their ecological myths. It is too easy to speak ironically. Who knows what will have come out of our ecologism and out of our diverse and marginal movements a hundred years from now, should a strong common idea ever succeed in crystallizing them and in moving them beyond mere picturesqueness?

Because the "Middle Ages" have a historically exemplary quality, knowing them will transcend picturesqueness better and faster than raising a few goats. The "Middle Ages" really do possess an intrinsic character, both because they lasted for some time and because they ended. Whether one fixes their extreme limits in the fifth and fifteenth centuries or, like Jacques Le Goff, in the third and eighteenth, this essential fact remains: here is a period not impossible to delimit within the continuum of human time, using more or less consistent criteria; it is a period long enough to exist in our laboratories on a more than microscopic scale, yet limited enough that its traits can be ascribed to more than mere probability. Such factors justify a global consideration of that period.[3] Having said this, I will remove the quotation marks with which, up to this point, I have cautiously framed the expression *Middle Ages*.

Of course, one could say the same things about other periods, other cultures. But, for the aggregate that was our Middle Ages, we know the terminus, if not the ultimate ends. One could not say as much about the universe of the Mayans. The nonmodernity of the Middle Ages (which provides its picturesqueness) puts us in a position to study the functioning of a society effectively: how can one know the laws that govern a society if one cannot see how those laws at last malfunctioned and were laid aside?

For these reasons, the Middle Ages occupy within our memory that crucial, problematic place in which our great-grandfathers held Greek and Latin antiquity. They are available as a permanent referent, working by analogy or by contrast on the levels of rational discourse and of affective reaction, to illuminate this or that aspect of our own mutability and manipulability. This way of thinking is no doubt too facile to be completely innocent; it may be an imaginary construct, created by certain fears of our own. But allow yourself a free play of associations: what would you evoke, in ten random subjects, by using an expression (deprived of all context) like "return to the Middle Ages"? "Return to antiquity" would scarcely mean anything: at best, vague memories of false grandeur and will to power. By contrast, what the Middle Ages engender is a cluster of questions.

§ The Middle Ages and Ourselves

Why this shift of interest from antiquity to the Middle Ages, a presumably irreversible evolution? It cannot be explained simply by recognizing one effect of that change in the cultural landscape which has taken place, beneath our feet, in the last quarter century. Once again, we have to make distinctions: between the general and the specific, between the latent and the manifest.

Once, in evoking the disintegration of ancient customs, Ortega y Gasset said, in effect: "As men of today, we suddenly have the feeling that we have been left alone on the earth." It is almost certain that the growing success of historical themes in the mass entertainment industry is due in part to the decline in our belief in scientific progress, to the rehabilitation of foreign or archaic cultures, and to the need to replace yesterday's fantasies with a knowledge of those things about which learned specialists *assure* us that "it really happened like that." This is a *reassuring* way to form an idea of one's self and perhaps of one's own death. Who can tell what unconscious relations bind a society to what it thinks is its own past?

At the heart of the vast ensemble of stories and images we absorb in this way, those which come down from the Middle Ages enjoy a special status. To the mass of consumers, the techniques of historical research have become impenetrable, impossible to grasp without misunderstanding. Alienated from the discipline as it is practiced, this mass audience finds in its own incapacities at least the possibility of forging a new affective bond with a past whose image may be distorted, but whose echoes are not quite extinguished in the sensibility or memory. More than other past eras, the Middle Ages appear to this audience as the soil from which spring its deep biological and psychic roots.[4] By contrast, the classicism imposed by official culture is rejected, along with the myth of antiquity, by the mass counterculture. In the Middle Ages it senses a "before" that is nearer at hand, less orderly, more primitive, one in which modern regional cultural movements hope to discover a vein that antedates the great standardization. This situation lends itself to certain abuses, which a few offended minds may deplore. It nonetheless constitutes for professional medievalists the sociological foundations of their activities. From it flow a certain number of obligations, of which, unfortunately, they are not always aware, and to which I will return.

Moreover, the relationships that arise in this way are complex and not always easy to assume. I will use the example of medieval "literary" texts. Chivalric romances, *fabliaux*, dramatic works, lyric poetry, and numerous other works of the twelfth, thirteenth, and fourteenth centuries have been translated in the last twenty years, and sometimes fairly widely distributed. Despite all they lose in translation, they have found readers. On one level, reading them satisfies a need for escape and, at the same time, a spontaneous wish for contact with an Other who, as we vaguely sense, resembles us in some way. "Each era," wrote Friedell thirty years ago, "forms its own idea of the past, one which typifies its own style of historical consciousness. . . . All history is chronicle, epic, myth, and, as such, the product of our capacity for intellectual synthesis, our power of imagination, our sense of the cosmos."[5]

Because of habits ingrained in a certain number of our contemporaries, all this results in a very reductive vision of the Middle Ages. For a long time (and perhaps it is still the case) this reductiveness forced the most astute practitioners of literary criticism to look upon the old texts with suspicion. Nevertheless, some medievalists in recent years have ventured beyond mere philological decoding and begun to decipher the great hieroglyphic monument that is "medieval literature." In this way, they have aroused new and more valid motivations to justify the relative popularity of their object of study. From one day to the next they have created the basis of a popularity that could be even wider, but better founded and therefore more fruitful.

Meantime, where the larger public is concerned, these medievalists have the task of offering a necessary initiation, fairly flexible and humble, but uncompromising. First of all they must invent some method of presenting the texts which is free of the servitudes of straight translation but which does not substitute those of the gloss. Various ventures of this sort are now in progress.

Where the critics are concerned, things have moved more rapidly, and a process of osmosis has already set in between various areas of speculation and research. It seems to me that a diffuse realization is spreading among specialists devoted to texts: the specific problems posed by medieval poetry and writing converge with what we used to call "modernity," from beyond the long, distinctive stretch of centuries labeled "classic." The latter, in fact, had constituted in literary discourse a particular system of values dominated and governed by one that passed, at least publicly, for the highest: "readability," as Roland Barthes defined the term. In medieval vernacular culture, up until the thirteenth century and even later, these values were unknown: and during the last hundred years, the classical system, bit by bit, has disintegrated for us. We find ourselves back in the same line of sight as the author of the *Romance of the Rose*, if not Guillaume de Machaut or Villon. One may, for pedagogical purposes, push the resemblance to the point of paradox. Nonetheless, the bare fact stands.

At the same time, the progress of ethnology is opening the horizon to numerous perceptible analogies between feudal Europe and some less developed, or otherwise developed, contemporary societies. Though the validity of these analogies may be debatable, they sometimes allow a useful renewal of historical perspective: for example, with respect to our texts, all the observations that have been made in the last thirty years or so on the functioning of oral traditions.[6] About this point, skepticism on the part of many medievalists has not prevented others (myself among them) from attempting a redefinition of medieval "textuality" based on such observations.

The Middle Ages created, from heterogeneous elements, the languages we speak today. It forged most of the discourses that we use and that give form to our instincts and thoughts. This has been said for a long time now, though with insufficient nuance, about our discourse of love. It ought to be said of our political, even economic, discourse, and the multiple forms of what Pierre Legendre calls "canonical discourse," which claims that everything human may be encompassed by science and the law—the tendency that continues to characterize many of our ways of speaking, including psychoanalysis.[7] Such facts reinforce the primitive intuition of a wider and wider public, anxious to shed as much light as possible on its own origins. Such a feeling is justified by the facts precisely inasmuch as they require a readjustment of medieval studies which, while not rejecting the intuition, may correct its misapprehensions.

For just this reason, in the recent work of specialists, scattered signs abound that there is a new self-awareness in the study, for its own sake, of medieval "literary" texts, a study that is tending to problemize itself as discourse.[8] It is problemizing the very notions on which its practice is based, such as those of form and meaning, breaking the circle that up to now has ensured, amid widespread indifference, "an infinite reproduction of formal distinctions just at the time when a new erudition was modifying their content."[9] The risks of all this are not negligible. But why not take them? Certain "multiple readings" attempted by well-intentioned medievalists result in an amalgam of contradictions and truisms: everything means everything, a perspective not so much universal as millenarian. Never mind; we are on the eve of a general mutation in our field. To accomplish it requires, above and beyond a rereading of the texts, a posing of the questions that will find in the texts themselves an answer that is pertinent and capable of bringing those texts to life.[10]

§ The Crisis

So the naive observer might suppose that all is well with the medievalists. There they go, three sheets to the wind, sailing toward a lyrical tomorrow.

Let us leave this naive observer to his marvelings; among ourselves we know full well what they are worth.

Simple honesty constrains us to pose a preliminary question: Have those factors that have led to the recent well-known advances in the human sciences as a whole, really had a profound effect on medieval studies? Or have the latter, despite a few apparent indices, lagged to a degree that may be difficult to evaluate?[11]

Considering medieval studies as a homogeneous whole, the balance sheet is certainly positive. But distinguishing their various sectors, we must acknowledge grave discrepancies. The study of literary texts, despite the signs I have mentioned, still has dusty and old-fashioned qualities discarded a good while ago by social history and the analysis of economic structures. The "history of medieval literature" seems something like the poor cousin of medieval studies, due, no doubt, to the specific nature òf its objects. That is precisely what prompts me to write this book.

How many works devoted to medieval literature give the reassuring impression that their author believes what he says? Very few. The reader often receives the opposite impression, that a bit of bad conscience is lurking somewhere: that the learned author whose prose he is reading is incessantly seeking alibis, because, even in his own eyes, to be a medievalist is not a self-evident achievement.[12]

But what is a self-evident achievement amid the urgent personal and collective problems assailing us today? The misery of the world is never a valid excuse for sidestepping one's concrete tasks. It does not free us of the obligation to work toward that opening which will have to be made one day, perhaps at our peril, starting with whatever crack we may succeed in making, in order to break the idealist hermeneutic circle and to force the discipline to renew its contents.

The unsatisfactory state of our field is not due solely to external circumstances or to human banality. It is engendered by certain tensions, at times irreducible, inherent in our discipline and essential to our ways of thinking and acting. In fact, whether or not they wish it, medievalists stand today at the point where several antinomic series converge. Some, of a very general nature, affect more or less all the human sciences. Others are specific to medieval studies. Still others belong to the study of medieval literatures.

The cultural backdrop against which this problematic defines itself is none other than a crisis of our language, provoked by the delayed discovery, in our century, of certain obvious truths affecting not only particular disciplines but the whole intellectual domain.

Whatever I say, in speaking about any "thing," remains exterior to that thing, and all the more inadequate to the concept of it which I elaborate while speaking. The critical language I use, that is, the "method" that guides me, aims (in the best of instances) to reduce this inadequacy by diminishing the extent of the exteriority: an ideal goal, never attained. Between the method which attempts to grasp the "thing," and the process, or practice, which produced that thing, there is not so much a distance as a radical difference, depending on the nature of the energy invested and the work accomplished.

If the "thing" is a text, the method consists of what I would call a *discourse-on*, whose relation to the text is one of application. Now, the practice that constituted, in the past, the same text, was a *discourse-in* (a relation of localization) and a *discourse-by* (a relation of cause and of instrument). Whence a double opposition, of which at least one (on/by) is never resolved, because *on* tends to establish taxonomies, while *by*, referring to production itself, tends to annul rational clarifications.

The linguistically inspired methods that prevailed for two decades in so-called literary research "discoursed on." But beginning several years ago, we have returned, not without problems or arguments, to the perception of what was for a long time (especially in the Middle Ages) a commonplace truth: one does not speak *about* writing; one writes.

Whence, among our contemporaries, our colleagues, even our

circles of medievalists, a sort of awareness has arisen shamefaced, veiled, sometimes disguised as aggressiveness, but nonetheless increasingly evident. There is a self-questioning of language, compelled to recognize itself for what it is: the repository of something unknown that creates us, and yet the dissimulator of this same unknown; but a repository that continually betrays itself, and an inept dissimulator. Thus, it constitutes the locus of our ambiguities, our denials, and at the same time makes up the stuff of our fantasies, the utopia of our dreams.

That is why, for the time being, there is no method in the strict sense of the term. What remains of it, or passes for it, is an uncertain number of relatively contradictory propositions, stating principles which, in the current state of our thinking, are as difficult to refute as to coordinate in a logical synthesis. We sense, on the one hand, the necessity of "sticking to the facts," perceived in their own cultural conditions, and, on the other hand, the necessity to integrate our reading of those facts with our own cultural functioning. We have become aware of the fundamentally historical nature of the human sciences, but aware also of that impasse which has been reached by the philosophy of history. We feel more and more clearly the urgent need not to sever the semiological aspect of the sign from the interpretation of the meaning; but we cannot ignore the tendency, deeply rooted in philological practice (which nothing has yet allowed us to put aside), to refuse whatever is separate from the letter, to deny that the "rest" is analyzable or even worthy of critical consideration.[13]

These epistemological antinomies are still today, for many of us, augmented by the weight of mental habits inherited from the nineteenth century: a sort of inability to tear ourselves away from an unexamined positivism, taken to be the very pattern of intellectual rectitude but operating on the basis of carefully hidden premises founded on the socio-historical conditions under which our discipline gradually took shape, simultaneously with the rise of modern bourgeois states. I will return to this aspect of our problem. Thus, on the methodological plane, three or four generations of researchers were governed by the four prejudices denounced by Fichant:[14] the "analytic" prejudice, reducing the whole to its elements, independently of the coherence that generates their meaning; the "teleological," reducing what came before to an anticipation of what came after; the "empirical," reducing "science" to the accumulation of "truths" reusable as such; and finally the "nominalist," reducing the concept to the word, that is to say, mythologizing a terminology.

All these prejudices together composed what was called "objectivity," considered as a high moral value, maintained at the cost of a true intellectual ascesis and adhered to in all good faith by those who were my mentors, sometimes in the noblest sense of the word: Edmond Faral, with his dry, distinguished manner and his aseptic language, who was good enough to encourage my early efforts although they were unfaithful to his teachings; Karl Voretzsch, proud of the imperial title of "Geheimrat" which made up for his small size, who was said to have boasted, in August 1914, that he would soon enter conquered Arles at the head of the Provençal regiment; Walter von Wartburg, who knew everything but who had only a few, rather narrow ideas, and who left to his memory alone the task of structuring knowledge; Robert Bossuat, who in 1935 gave me a 2 out of 20 on my Old French examination. That is not my motive for writing these lines! But none of these details are "objectively" insignificant.

However, we know today that texts do not lend themselves to being grasped, and that no critical activity can, or should, attempt this "objectivity" from the outset. Far from it. Criticism will achieve some degree of coherence only by questioning those very conditions that make its practice possible, those modalities of interference between the text and the subjectivity of the critic.[15]

§ The Medievalist Institution

From all this come our troubles, our hesitations, and the occasional discrepancies in our research, not to say the incoherence of the results obtained. Whence, at times when fatigue overtakes us, or a failure momentarily blocks us, this feeling of uselessness, even fright, in the face of that jumble which seems to characterize our bibliographies.

What we lack is an idea of the ultimate ends of our work, as well as an idea of the generative laws of our discourse. Perhaps our predecessors had this idea and we have lost it. But it would be useless, in any event, to borrow it back from the learned men of the past; it could not function unless it were our own. And, to all appearances, we have been removed, for fifty years, from the old, traditional world of generations leaning on one another's shoulders. For us, it falls to each generation to redefine everything according to the notion it has of itself.

From all this, in our hours of distress, comes the feeling of abandonment that besets us. Like Ortega y Gasset's people, we have been left alone on the earth . . . of medieval studies! We have lost (the literary specialists more than others) the strong support on which our mentors leaned: this "body of medievalists" about which Henri-Irénée Marrou spoke, only a quarter century ago, as he leaned his head on his long, dry hand, looking like a Church Father painted by El Greco. This "body" was so cohesive, so thoroughly grafted, in Europe and America, onto university administrations, that one could speak without much contradiction of the Medievalist Institution.[16]

Diverse, certainly, thanks to the wide variety of talents that are active within it, this Institution has in fact remained massive up to recent times, with an ensemble of forms and roles comprising its agents, with appropriate rules and language, with a coded transmission of the heritage. There has been an absence, not to say a refusal, of any reflection on the Institution itself which might relativize it. . . . However, for some time now, heterogeneous movements have been discernible within it. There remain, projecting a network of partial unities onto this heterogeneity, a small number of simplified schemas, maintained in a few bastions, not innocently but stubbornly. Even there, no doubt, many concepts have evolved; a part of the vocabulary has been renewed. But essentially, this moribund institutional discourse moves in a direction contrary to that of medieval Christianity, which, beneath all the stability of its rhetoric, was constantly in motion. Still apparently enthroned in the center of our horizon, but in fact marginalized, the Institution, or what is left of it, is little more than a ghetto now, and refuge for those among us who are the least gifted with an aptitude for communication, therefore the least apt to respond to the needs of a changed world.

For all this, the Institution as such does not exist out of any vital necessity. On the contrary, as we observe in other research fields, creative thinking often takes place outside it. The only true vital necessity is the incessant redefinition that I have already described. It is the reexamination, at all times, of the relation that exists between the old text and its erudite reader; it is the questioning of the way of knowledge that we can adopt in the 1980s with respect to the object we propose to study. This inquiry also concerns the knowledge that the Middle Ages had of itself, and the ways we can find of coming to know that knowledge.

This is what I meant when I spoke of the ultimate ends of our studies, and about the generative laws of our discourse: I understand these terms in a pragmatic perspective. Perhaps I should say an *ethical* one, related to some reciprocal, explicit link between knowledge, will, possibility, and action. One could never define that link once and for all; still less could one hold it in place. Humanist ethics have become as foreign to our universe as the economic structures of the eleventh century. We have lost that utopian desire that led our forebears to lay claim, in their every enterprise, to the world of tomorrow by evoking the world of yesterday. It has been said before: the past has ceased to guarantee the future, and our social movements themselves are mainly an affirmation of our existence in the here and now.

§§§·

A Question of Identity

Initially, there are a few things to ask the medievalist, particularly the specialist in "literary" texts: Is the mode of knowledge that he proposes to attain identifiable as such? How can it be defined in its specificity? Does his field of activity constitute an epistemological field unified by presuppositions that can be analyzed?

One can, in a summary way, distinguish three variables among the elements of our research: the medievalist himself (whom I will call the "critical reader"), that which he intends to read, and the method of reading that mediates the relationship thus established. Only an examination of these variables—their nature and the extent of their transformation—will permit us at least to map out some answers.

In more concrete terms, one may ask if the essential traits of our discipline stem from the (professional?) quality of those who practice it, from the language they use, or from the point of view they adopt, that is, from their way of dividing up the continuity of the real. Probably it is from all these together. Traditionally, the difficulty was short-circuited by stating that what defined a study was its object. But today we are no longer justified in clinging to that positivist prejudice which hypostasized the object.

In what follows I will take up those three factors. The last two, which are hard to dissociate, will constitute the heart of this book. The first, however, despite its capital importance, can be dealt with more briefly.

It is a truism (though less of one than we may think) that the excellence of a given piece of research depends in large part on the intellectual capacities and the honesty of the researcher, and the validity of a reading on the intelligence and sensibility of the reader. No one would deny the long-term impact effected in our discipline at certain times by the major personal traits of some scholar who managed to imprint upon it, as it were, the features of his own character. The work of the gentle Auerbach, with his large eyes and his expression of timid goodness, marked a generation, otherwise but no less than the work of the brilliant Spitzer, that great conversationalist, self-confident and beloved by women. One could cite many other names; I am only recalling a few impressions to which I was particularly sensitive because of the happenstances of my career. And of the many whom I have known, I prefer to evoke only those who are now among the dead.

In any case, all this is more than anecdotal. Above and beyond his individual gifts, each one of these scholars constituted—each one of us constitutes—the convergence of certain cultural determinants, some of which have, as much as possible, been consciously assumed and thereby made productive, others of which remain hidden or denied and are therefore all the more disruptive. Either way, they have their effect. In speaking of the Middle Ages, I can only speak from what happens to be my place in the sun: a place circumscribed as much by the intellectual demands of the day as by the socio-historic conditions that engender them.

H. R. Jauss, in tracing, by way of example, the history of studies on the epic, shows how in Germany its phases emerged successively from the ideological preoccupations of a few researchers: at the beginning of this century Becker was calling into question the evolutionary paradigm; in the thirties Curtius, wishing to construct a unified image of European poetry, universalized the values of rhetoric; after 1950 the influence of the Swiss Jean Rychner linked the problem with that of oral traditions, as defined by Parry's American school; finally, in 1975, A. Adler proposed that the ensemble of French medieval epics be read as a synchronic but shifting web of signs that refer to the contradictions of feudal society. J. Le Goff, for his part, has written the story of Michelet and those variations in his conception of the Middle Ages which were imposed by the changing events he himself was living through.[17]

There are many "places in the sun," and as many ways to find oneself in one's place—and to feel its uncertainty. It is not the same "from where I stand" that people used to refer to; or, if it is the same, it has another meaning, because even uncertainty is a place to stand.

To approach the same problem in another way: we speak well only about things we know concern us personally, about things we love, perhaps. Every relationship we maintain with a text involves some latent eroticism. Only this dynamism puts the critical reader in a situation comparable to that of the medieval reader or listener, whose whole body, not only his visual and auditory faculties, was engaged in the reception of the text.

Thus, the personal factor in our studies is defined primarily within the order of desire. If my discourse must consist in pronouncing a "true" proposition about its object, what, then (once I am beyond the erudite, always debatable phase of the research) is this "truth" but a profound accord, consoling and joyful, between the desire that brings *me* to *my* object, and the understanding that *I* acquire of it? My "truth" implicates *me* at the same time as *my* object—though we must not, at any moment, mistake ourselves; that trust is only a place of transition: between me and an Other, made believable, despite absence, by my discourse; placed in me and in you to whom I speak while remaining irrevocably hidden.

However, nothing is solved by all this, and along the way we will have come upon a lot of traps, into which many have fallen. When we set off, one day in our youth, in quest of that elusive object, the medieval text, our motive was an interest in the history of the past: curiosity, of course, but also a need for warmth, the memory of a matrix. But, as everyone knows, we do not return to the womb that bore us. So, without realizing it, we deny our desire, and give in to the temptation of hunting for old things. Erudition becomes the refuge of many a failed Oedipus.

§ History and Practice

In the present state of our studies, their object, as we have repeatedly heard, is produced by the discourse upon it, whose aim is to outline it within the heart of a continuous, more or less vast sector of the universe: a sector that has been roughly isolated a priori by virtue of empirical observations subject to perpetual revision. Henri Poincaré said long ago that "the method lies in one's choice of the facts."

Thus, the object of a critical reading is both a text and an event. As a text, it is materially identifiable; as an event, it is not given, but chosen. This choice cannot be innocent. It supposes a prior interpretation and a present interest: but nothing is more easily camouflaged than those two factors. Our task will be to make them manifest and to answer for their consequences; to state thus, unequivocally, that the event and the language by which it is spoken define one another. Together, they constitute a practice, a process, and a work, the elaboration of a discipline, involving a qualitative leap that moves us from a relatively passive phase (the inquiry: that which in ancient Greek was called *historia*), into a dramatic operation, whose purpose can only be to make us hear a voice.

This voice can easily be stifled by hidden presuppositions (in the order of prior interpretation and present interest) just when it is about to break the silence. Thus, in the last few years naive application of borrowed notions, such as that of "writing," led many medievalists, in all good faith, to distort, if not to caricature, the object which they thought they were grasping. Doubtless because they placed themselves within the history of those texts, these scholars took as univocal and homogeneous that which, being culturally conditioned, can only be, in the long perspective of time, heterogeneous and ambiguous.

Here is another example. Distortions that weaken the erudite heritage left us by our predecessors stem in part from their very conception of a "medieval literature"—designating by a term derived from *littera* the ensemble of texts whose transmission was (as we must insist) principally oral, founded on the proximity of the word, inseparable from its place and from the body from which it emanates, inseparable too from those who hear it, along an intermittent time-line, out of a past in which a new meaning, fragmented and never identical to itself, is periodically re-formed.

Quite apart from this *contradictio in terminis*, "literature" was, until the seventeenth century, hardly ever, and only bit by bit, identified as a particular class of discourse. The notion was created, in the heart of existing traditions, by the imposition of several schemes of thought that were new then and functioned in a hidden way as critical parameters: the idea of an autonomous speaking "subject," of the possibility of grasping the other, the conception of a reified "object," the preeminence granted to the referentiality of language, and, simultaneously, to fiction; the presupposition of the supratemporality of a certain type of discourse, socially transcendent, suspended in empty space. We know today that such a discourse does not exist, any more than does a historiography whose way of conceiving past reality has no special textual effect. Whence the birth of the imperative category of "literary," which was made the bearer of values that the Middle Ages had attributed—somewhat vaguely—to the antique *auctores*, a new category that subsumed, on its own level, all aspects of knowledge.

A typically "modern" field of study offered itself to critical reflection; it included both structural description and functional examination. Romanticism, by pushing this activity in an idealist direction, attempted to designate a "literary absolute" in the years when medieval studies were taking shape.[18] Today, whatever may be the diversity in theoretical orientation, no part of this conceptual ensemble remains unproblematic. Barthes, in his inaugural lecture at the Collège de France, defined "literature" as a way of luring language away from power relationships, as a "complex graph of the traces of a practice." It could not be more aptly stated.

How many medievalists have sufficiently realized this? To be sure, old-fashioned medievalism entered only halfway into the system; but if the new generation was wary, it was only from empirical motives, under the influence of the "neogrammarians," for whom all that was ever written has the status of raw linguistic data. The result was that any text whatever, copied between the ninth and fifteen centuries, found its place in "medieval literature" as well as in "history of the language." This pseudo-principle was subject to exceptions that were never explained: archival texts such as acts of donation were excluded, but not works of vulgarization designed to communicate fragments of clerical learning to the lay public. Moreover, nothing of that which, on the linguistic level, makes for the functional specificity of texts was taken into consideration.

Medievalists nonetheless remained guests of honor in the literary institution, well established by that time. Hiding from themselves the incoherence of their attitudes, they adopted the presuppositions of the Rule: the distinction between an inside and an outside (infinitely reducible oppositions: popular vs. learned, paraliterary vs. literary, and so on); the idea of a particular knowledge, a suprapersonal tradition incessantly enriched with discoveries and judgments accumulated in the eternity of Progress.

Thus, for our mentors, to speak of "literature" came down to declaring the fundamental conformity of our ancient poems with that which a well-bred person might read in the Paris or the Vienna of 1900. Biased without realizing it, erudition did away with history in order to awaken (surreptitiously) the pleasure of the aesthete.

But these poems, preserved thanks to the labor of scribes, are for us now only texts, nothing more, and force us to compare our own reading and speech with a practice that is no longer ours. Thus, the word that we decipher within them circumscribes a nonexistent place in us. But about these contradictions, in 1900 (and even in 1950!) no one said a word—unless perhaps the great Don Ramon, the venerable Menendez Pidal, whose solitary voice (already faint by the time I had begun to wake up to these problems) spoke to us of an entirely poeticized history, and of a poetry unthinkable otherwise than as history.

At the extreme ends of the chain: on the one hand, the singer Taillefer or the romancer Chrétien de Troyes; on the other, you and me. Further: on the one hand, the way in which the *Chanson de Roland* was received by the warriors at Hastings (a dubious anecdote, but never mind that for now), or *Le Chevalier au lion* by the lords and ladies gathered before the lectern of a reader; on the other hand, my reading and the one to which, as mediator, I invite you. Between these extremes, the text: historicized as words pronounced in the eleventh or twelfth century; yet, as a formal composition, in a way transhistorical—perceptible at once, then, in a chronological verticality *and* in a transcultural horizontality.

The idea of a practice is multiple: here as there, from production to reception, by communication, the same dialectic, inversely symmetrical, on both sides of a slice of history. But I am still oversimplifying: with very rare exceptions, we are observing not one but two communications, different in nature, at each end of the chronological distance:

1. original communication (production and reception), generally beyond the limits of our gaze;

2. mediated communication I (production and reception of the manuscript or manuscripts);

[a chronological gap, generally several centuries, during which there may intervene an indeterminate number of communications socio-historically different from numbers 1, 2, 3, and 4];

3. mediated communication II (produced by the scholar and received by a specialized clientele, typified in the teaching phase);

4. communication put in a form consumable today (aimed at reception by all interested individuals).

Thus, there are not three terms but at least twelve that enter into consideration, each involving its own variables, that is, its own way of being historical.

The ideal would be to grasp, at each of the constituent phases in my schema, the tradition of a textual practice, the complex act that produced an intention as well as a word, an inherent signifying effect, and a response. Each of these terms presents great complexity, predetermined as it is within social discourse and by ideological factors. The German critics of the "School of Constance" speak today, in this sense, of "concretization" and declare that the meaning of a text is defined as the historical sequence of its concretizations. With medieval texts, this historical sequence is full of gaps! A matter of insufficient documentation; in fact, most of the lines in our diagrams have to be dotted ones. The necessity remains for us medievalists to maintain, in the face of all apparent impossibilities, two affirmations of principle: (1) every text supposes the existence of a long series of interpersonal relations, dialogic, probably quite shifting, in the course of time articulated on the basis of that text; (2) it is by means of these relations that history becomes implicated in the debate.

This necessity cannot but complicate the work of erudition. But what is to be done about it? Some of the most illustrious medieval texts, for example, El Cid, Flamenca, or the Chanson de Guillaume d'Orange, have only come to us thanks to a single manuscript, often incomplete or in poor condition. By what expedient can we glimpse what may have been its successive concretizations? This difficulty, in extreme cases, ends by inspiring doubts about the text's very authenticity: the Slavists are still debating over the Song of Igor's Campaign.

True, fortune sometimes smiles on us. In the fifties, Stern and then García Gómez revealed to us a whole body of Andalusian poetry from the eleventh, twelfth, and thirteenth centuries (lost until then in Hebraic or Arab manuscripts), its existence having been vaguely presumed by a few audacious specialists. However, the Italian medievalist L. Renzi, only twenty years ago, reflecting on our textual documentation, could still compare the great French period from 1150 to 1200 to an abandoned city that the inhabitants had left open to all the insults of time, where, of all the crumbled monuments, only a few fragments of wall remain. . . . This view errs by excessive pessimism. But it does suggest that we should equip ourselves as archeologists rather than as tourists. Furnished with a battery of tools, manual and intellectual, and with enough sensitivity to discern where that now broken line was leading, to see which way was pointed that sculpted arrow you just picked up among the thorns.

When a text has been identified, published, and more or less situated in a chronology, analogous problems arise on another level. It is tempting (and today, I think, necessary), in order to illuminate the dialogic function we are supposing, to borrow the critical resources of psychoanalysis. But (as experience proves all too well!) nothing is really resolved by that, because we lack information on a fundamental point: even if we admit that the human unconscious has always functioned in a more or less identical manner, is it not possible that history, on the scale of long time spans, has displaced the blurred borderline where consciousness takes root in the unconscious, in opposition to it, and has shifted the place where symptoms emerge?[19]

§ The Other

Thus, for a few years now the question to which I have already alluded has been raised: the question of the otherness of the Middle Ages.

Nothing can truly compensate for the chronological distance that separates the medievalist from his object. This fact has weighty consequences. In me, on the one hand, and, on the other, in the object of my desire, two historical realities confront one another, irreconcilable despite any specious resemblances. A radical duplicity which (according to Jauss) itself makes for the interest and, for us, the value of medieval studies: the determination of the otherness of the Middle Ages (definable both on the axis of time spans and on the level of structures) should provoke in us the perception of an identity and should make its components explicit.

An optimistic view, to be sure, which perhaps simplifies somewhat the available facts: *Otherness*, whatever its Hegelian resonances may be, refers to diverse situations and may be interpreted in several ways, in the perspective of a long but continuous history, or in that of an abrupt break between two temporal fragments. Just this sort of break, mythicized, was called, by the nineteenth-century medievalists, the Renaissance. . . .

More generally, one may distinguish an absolute otherness, produced by any confrontation between a subject and an object. This belongs to the existential order and is not what we are speaking about here. It goes without saying; yet, it can be made dramatic by circumstances. For the historian or the ethnologist (the medievalist shares some qualities of one and the other), it manifests itself at times as radical otherness, excluding any feeling of belonging to a common universe, at times as relative otherness, inviting translation and engendering the desire to learn the language of the Other, or, to borrow a word from Jean Massin, the Stranger.

The otherness of the Middle Ages, in this sense, is more relative than that of the primitive world or, for Westerners, that of ancient China. Our Middle Ages include a past that is both close and distant, foreign but familiar: isn't that a traditional definition of the "neighbor," the person whom, by turns, we exploit and love? Whence a tendency to idealize this "Middle" Ages, the stronger because it is deeply rooted in a diffuse collective sensibility, more so than the tendency of an Egyptologist to idealize the empire of Amenophis, or the ethnologist the society of the Trobrianders. The Middle Ages belong to our history: belong to us, in a very special way, because biologically and culturally we are their direct descendants.

Nonetheless, on the level of methodological principles we cannot make gradations. Any text coming from a former epoch must in a fundamental way be received as one coming from a universe in which we by no means participate. Any analogy between that universe and ours must be supposed illusory (until there is explicit proof of the contrary), which does not mean that pertinent analogies do not exist.

The only doubtful question here is: What is a former time? Starting at what point does age engender historical otherness? Endless discussions could be undertaken on this point. The rhythms of history, as we have learned from Braudel, do not all have the same amplitude. However, the case of our Middle Ages is, on the whole, less debatable than would be that of the French seventeenth century. Despite some marginalized survivals in our attitudes and mores, there is a consensus among us that we can declare the Middle Ages to be a former time. Whence the necessity for medievalists to give a privileged status, in their awareness of their object, to marks of the distance that separates them from it.

Nevertheless, it is not the feeling of otherness per se that creates the interest, but the relationship that the medievalist establishes between the Stranger and us, while preventing a fallacious identification between subject and object. The more strongly we are implicated in this relationship, the more our interest grows, to the point, one day, of engaging our whole existence. But the strength of this relationship depends not so much on the will of individuals (here, of critical readers) as on a socio-historical situation. I don't think I am deluding myself in stating that in the 1980s the Middle Ages are, from the point of view of our social practices and ideologies, more actual than they were in the 1880s.

Whence, perhaps, in part, the discomfort of our position.

Joining to chronological distance an apparently close anthropological link with today's observer, the field of medieval studies entails a danger that we are only beginning to appreciate: the deceptive ease with which this *déjà vu* can be muffled as it comes in the door, and then become caught in our own systems of resemblances. But the sole chance of survival for our discipline lies in our repeatedly calling into question the proximity of the Middle Ages, not in order to affirm what remains eternally obvious, but in order to create an interest in this *déjà vu* as such. We forget this sometimes, when elated by the temptations of renewal.

These terms pose a problem of interpretation not altogether dissimilar to the one which the thirteenth century resolved, according to its own intellectual tendencies, in its reading of Aristotle. The problem demands that we abandon those prejudices (at times hard to perceive) formed at the time when our discipline was founded, by analogy or naive contrast to the idea that the nineteenth century had of itself. We can no longer fail to take certain things into account: the high degree of semioticity of a culture—the Middle Ages—which thought of itself as an immense network of signs; the fact that the conventional character of medieval art implies a near-Platonic comprehension of the Chain of Resemblances, proceeding from absolute Identity to perfect Otherness; the fact that, beneath the cover of this tradition, the rhythm of history in the eleventh, twelfth, and thirteenth centuries was a rapid one, contrary to a widely held opinion; the fact that this period was characterized not so much by a lack of technological advance as by ignorance of the scientific status of mathematics. . . . One could easily multiply such examples.[20]

In every instance of our reading we assume the primacy of history in two ways, inasmuch as that word designates a process, a mode of being and of signifying events and structures, and inasmuch as it designates a mode of perception and of description of lived reality implied in our present. . . . The danger which threatens us here (and which was seldom avoided by the first generations of medievalists) would be to reduce these factors, on the one hand to a simple sequence of events, on the other, to an annalistic discourse. At the least, even when a methodological illusion led, in the examination of our texts, to a denial of their history, the latter was not abolished. It was the "natural milieu" (in about the same sense as the term is used in ecology) of everything that in the course of time was said, written, heard, or read, a milieu that allows man (allows the text) to live, *and* against which he creates himself. At the same time, history, in common with the other human sciences, functions among us today in the same way as myths did in traditional societies. There is no end to it all.

True, our situation lacks clarity. We critical readers have not completely freed ourselves from the romantic conception according to which history basically is the history of culture in the restricted sense of the word. However, our colleagues among the historians of institutions and of mores are working now in the field of socioeconomic facts; and the solidity of their information, like the breadth of the problems they confront, has allowed several of them to occupy a central place on the horizon of our concerns: Duby and Le Goff in France, Tenenti and Cipolla in Italy, Norbert Elias in Germany, John Baldwin in the United States. . . . Too much reciprocal ignorance still intervenes between them and us, the readers of texts, along with misunderstandings that we must overcome—without taking on scientistic pretensions.

In critical reading, as in many other disciplines, when it comes to things that escape formalization, if not precise measurement, we commonly hear: "That is explainable historically." Thus, history is invoked as the substitute for a tool that would have nailed the "object" once and for all to the board and severed the link between it and me. Thus we innocently proclaim, do we not, the irreducibility of history?[21]

§ Double Historicity

There is no historical discourse any more than there is a scientific discourse. There was, over the centuries, a long series of discourses projecting onto the universe successive schemes engendered by our cultures and by the circumstances that determined them. Romanticism, to which we still have so many ties, formed (perhaps because it was tired of the old utopias) the idea of cyclic progressions, which justified comparing the *Chanson de Roland* to the *Iliad*. A. B. Lord and his disciples are doing that again today, but on premises and with intentions entirely foreign to romanticism, in the course of an inquiry into the sociological and poetic functioning of "living epic." So, whether in an obvious way or not, the least that each generation can attempt, to assure its survival, is to attach some of its own concepts to discourses that it has not itself pronounced.[22]

What, in this perspective, is a "fact"? Books, like that of J. Parain-Vial eighteen years ago, have been written on this theme. We are justified in wondering if this notion, which is being taken over by our positivists, does not result from the progressive erosion of a great medieval idea, one that may be seen taking shape in the Carolingian era, beginning with the work of John Scotus Eriugena: that history is a being, that this being possesses a form, and that this form may be represented. An emanation of being passes through the forms, redeeming chaos: whence the traditions by which they manifest themselves—monumental sculpture; illuminated, or "historiated," books; allegory. . . . What remains of the ontological density of these forms in our "historical fact," a concept so fragile that it lets any concept of cause slip away? Even entities like *state, people, nation, literature, culture, oeuvre,* which help us to situate those concepts and to make sense of them, constitute not givens so much as problems; and any problem today is, in turn, only one given of a more complex problem that incorporates it.

Therefore, it is not so much history as such that we must emphasize here as the respective historicities of the reader and his or her object:[23] an idea which was already emerging (against Croce?) around 1930 among the founders of *Annales,* and which stated that there is a reciprocity in our relation to the past. The idea of historicity, with reference to the specific quality of being-in-history as well as being-history, implies some appropriation of the real: it manifests itself on the level of type-situations, significant stages that lead a person to this appropriation; situations which, at times, can only be the contingent and immediate realization of a possible, inscribed in time.

Historicity is the trait which, in the study of ancient cultures, in the critical reading of ancient or medieval texts, characterizes

32

simultaneously, but separately and differently, the one who reads and that which is read. This situation does not change, regardless of whether or not the reader is aware of it. If we acknowledge, with the semioticians of Tartu, that history is a text that the social body communicates to itself while reacting to it, history locates itself both within this reading and in the production of new sentences generated by the reading.[24] The intervention of otherness more or less dissociates these terms, rendering them complex and hetero-geneous.

Thus, in the medievalist's critical reading, two historicities touch, without merging into one another. Just as any interpreta-tion of space is made on the basis of *here*, and that of the other on the basis of *I*, inversely, the antiquarian delusion which might lead one to speak of the past otherwise than on the basis of *now* would render outdated and futile whatever interpretation of it one might make.[25] I have myself, to some degree, apparently given in to this delusion by emphasizing too heavily, in my *Essai de poétique médiévale*, the function exerted by tradition in the Middle Ages. For one thing, the historicity of medieval texts could never be ex-plained thereby; for another, in this twentieth century can our own historicity permit us to read those texts as traditional ones?[26]

We steer a course between Scylla and Charybdis. The ultimate term we aim for is really to bring the ancient text into the present, that is, to integrate it into that historicity which is ours. The pitfall is that in doing so we may deny or obscure its own historicity: we may foreshorten the historical perspective and, by giving an achronic shape to the past, hide the specific traits of the present. It is this very pitfall that Eric Rohmer, for example, managed to avoid in his *Perceval*, where the manifest artifice engenders something like a second sense of the natural, one to which we have immediate access; where the fortuitous incompleteness of the Chrétien de Troyes text is functionalized in a final sequence immediately meaningful to all. Jacques Roubaud and Florence Delay have brought about another such miracle on a similar theme.

In medieval intellectual practice, the structures of thought constituted by the "liberal arts" effectively assured the dividing up of empirical reality, determined the event, designated the fact, while at the same time furnishing a basis for their interpretation.

Not taking account of this given would be as absurd as failing to go beyond it—as we have done too often. The liberal arts no longer exist for us: the human sciences have finally replaced them. Other events, other facts, other interpretive factors intervene: ours is the heavy task of translating them.

To interpret, to explain: this is to situate an object within a meaning. A text, especially if it is old, can circumvent that operation. It is ours to find the weak point, and perhaps to seduce the text. But no one is thereby authorized to pretend that the text has every possible meaning. In every instant of its life span, as long as it materially subsists, what it says is only a new vision, which successive readers may appropriate, of what it originally stated. Every modern hermeneutic, from Dilthey to Gadamer and Paul Ricoeur, has turned upon that problem.[27]

§ Language and History

To insert a text into history does not exhaust its potential for meaning. I have already evoked the shifting nature, in the course of time, of the dialogic relations established in and about any text. The problem involves many other givens, which, up until 1975, provoked many critical discussions, almost always about "literary" monuments subsequent to the Middle Ages. To be sure, what one says of any text also applies, in principle, to the medieval text: at least so it seems, and I think one can set aside the idea of a difference in *kind* between the texts. Nevertheless, the differences, on the level of modalities, appear such that one cannot prudently, in practice, base one's reading on the resemblances.

The object of our critical desire is a text or an ensemble of texts, from which emanate (as one must acknowledge a priori) an unforeseeable number of values. The historical questions that arise around the text present more unknowns than those associated with the historicity of plastic or musical forms. The textual monument is, in effect, a monument of language.

In fact, the study of "medieval literature" has for a century been continuously conjoined with linguistics—to be sure, at the cost of several misunderstandings and singular simplifications. In the serene times of a Gaston Paris, the "neogrammarians" traced the history of atomized facts, identified with an indisputable reality. (I will return to discuss the influence they exerted on our discipline, a pernicious one in the long run.) For them, language is only an aggregate. When, during Bédier's lifetime, Saussure overturned this perspective, he did it by rejecting history. More recently we came to know the illusory optimism that took linguistics as a pilot discipline and then attributed to it (not that the linguists themselves can be held responsible) a modeling function relative to all the human sciences.

That moment has passed. But there remain a few more or less assured principles:

1. The functioning of a text is not identical to that of language; however, the two are related.

2. The text fills a space, realizes potentialities, in relation to which the linguistic act as such stays in the background.

3. Language works in the text, as in the unconscious, by displacement and condensation.

4. Aesthetic information nonetheless passes through the codification of the message.

5. The text is an utterance; history is one part of the enunciation; and it can happen that, for us who are interested in old texts, only this part falls within the description, that is, within the meaning.

Here it would be proper to attenuate certain affirmations in my *Essai de poétique*, in which, around 1970, I maintained, without adequate nuance, that medieval poetry, like all poetry, far from imitating reality, takes itself as object. The idea of this perfect autoreferentiality has had its day. But two obvious points remain: one is that the primary reciprocal relation between the subject and its language is altered by the ideological investment practiced in the text; the other is that texts, one by one, like the collectivity of real discourse, are poured back into the language and, through it, into history, to the point, over the long term, of merging with them.

But before we can provide any kind of description of these antinomies, a question arises which will determine all future operations: What reciprocal link joins language with history? A fundamental question (even when one specifies it in terms like "the text and history"), it concerns, along with the whole domain of erudition, the totality of our epistemological presuppositions.

I might be accused of overdramatizing. A certain critical tradition has, in fact, a tendency to reduce the impact of the problem as I am posing it. One simply wants to ask: is this link an immediate one or not? Among medievalists, for instance,[28] we have the abundant literature of glosses on themes like the *chanson de geste* and history, or the Cathars and the troubadours.

The simplified procedures of a certain socio-criticism do not, in effect, work well on this fleeting reality, buried in languages to which we do not even have all the keys. Of course it is necessary to admit the existence of correspondences (yet to be defined) between the text and its historical context: these correspondences are more obvious in narrative texts, where the factor of verisimilitude transforms them into homologies by reproducing at least a few aspects of extratextual reality. But less important than those nuances is the nature of the correspondences and the level on which they function. The masterful experiment of Erich Köhler is one instance: for Köhler, the analysis of correspondences involves textual macrostructures and imaginative schemas, identified with an ideology; the courtly romance thus appears as the compensatory projection onto the screen of language of a type of society defined on the basis of this myth. . . . But the microstructures, it seems to me, reveal in the same texts, perceptible at all levels of the language, an intrusion into the discourse of temporality, of a dynamism from which come exchanges, transformations, and dispersions in space and time. But there flourished in the same period the sung poetry of the *trouvères*, whose discourse was, by contrast, achronic, circular, centripetal. There is, therefore, between these two sequences, a tension, if not a contradiction, definable precisely on the level of the text and radiating from it, incorporating the whole perspective of what is said and spoken about, and of surrounding circumstances.

Whether or not the link between the text and history is an immediate one, what counts is that the knowledge we have of the link is mediated twice, once by the objects that it isolates and once by the discourse that it uses to do so. Not one of these elements is exterior to language: the place for interpretation is at the heart of language, not in a previously intended meaning or in an exterior reference.

Ours is a delirious profession, as Valéry would have described it: the reality that supports and warrants our practice is enclosed in a forbidden zone which we cannot broach without forfeiting the reasons for our discourse.[29] The admirable complexity of what exists, the delicious interpenetration of all values, are ours to understand and, let us hope, to speak about, without ever leaving this small piece of earth on which our feet are placed, among the traces of words spoken by someone else, centuries ago, uttered, perhaps, for his deliverance, and for our joy.

The constraints created by this situation have only recently manifested themselves. For medievalists (and many others!) they define themselves in two ways at once: as the need for reflection (or, at the least, for broad and solid information) on the functionings of language, and as the necessity for a profound knowledge of the medieval languages. The second seems self-evident (and was for a long time the only one to be recognized); the first does not seem evident to everyone, but it holds all the same.... Whence the enormousness of the preparatory, or continuing, task for the critic of medieval texts. Perhaps it is this situation that explains the lag which has overtaken our field with respect to the criticism of modern texts as well as other sectors of medieval history. The historian of feudal institutions or of Romanesque sculpture does not share the discomfort of our position: we listen to the discourse of an invisible other who speaks to us from some deathbed (or some couch) of which the exact location is unknown to us; we attempt to distinguish in the fantasies of this stranger the echo of a voice which, somewhere, probes, knocks against the world's silence, begins again, is stifled.... As for the other world, it has neither voice nor language; the world is the Other of language. But we know it is there, present, its weight mingled with every articulation our ear perceives; it is there, transfigured.

§ The Horizon of Expectations

We must proceed indirectly: a frontal attack would crash against the wall of the text. Perhaps one of the ruses of this strategy resides in having recourse to the notion of the "theatricality" of the medieval text, which I proposed in 1972 and which served as a point of departure for my study of the Grands Rhétoriqueurs.[30] In effect, this notion permits us to integrate with the text itself, in at least one of its best-differentiated aspects, the "natural milieu" to which it belonged. Thus, in a fairly broad zone of concrete reality submitted to study, internal analysis joins with the analysis of a social function.

In this way the point of view that I adopted strongly resembled, as I intended it to, the one suggested by work done at the Constance School under the name "aesthetics of reception." It attempts to perceive, within the text, a man, not, of course, as the object of knowledge, but rather as the cause, effect, and circuit of all signification; and, through him, to perceive a socialized being, a locus of formation for nonatomizable products, for units of energy, for perpetual movement and exchange.[31]

That, or nearly that, was the course recommended in the past, in another language, by Mukařovsky when he defined the aesthetic function of the work as an empty principle, organizing and dynamizing the other functions of language. This aesthetic, or poetic function, as critics close to Jauss now specify, is constituted at the cost of negating other functions, yet does not detach its gaze from the reality that it has negated. In this way, the lived present, once aestheticized, transcends and overwhelms the original pragmatic situation: a distancing that others have attempted to measure more precisely, in terms of a heavily Hegelianized Marxism.[32]

I probably owe a few words of explanation on this point to those of my readers who have followed my work for a quarter century. I have, in fact, turned around this point in spiral fashion much of the time, and I am far from thinking I have finally reached it! My Histoire littéraire de la France médiévale (1954) proposed the principle of an intimate relationship between the text and the extratextual: incapable of defining it, I at least acknowledged that it was the only thing that made possible a classification of the texts. *Langues et techniques poétiques* (1963) left those relationships implicit and attempted to perceive the mode of existence of the texts in the heart of a language seen as constantly evolving. In *Essai de poétique médiévale* (1972), I defined more explicitly this matrix of language both as structure and as genesis; but it seems to me that the bond between these two lines of argument did not hold well, whence an uncertain vacillation from one to the other, which could be interpreted as a barely tempered, orthodox structuralism. *Le Masque et la lumière* (1978) offered me an opportunity to overcome this contradiction: on the one hand, by setting aside any notion of causality, on the other hand by endeavoring to isolate, on several levels of entrenchment, the relations maintained by the texts, in an external way with chronicity, in an intrinsic way with the factors of their historicity, and in a dynamic way with the future, inasmuch as one can say that they, in turn, engendered history.

I am still far from the mark. What now? Now, perhaps, a long detour through the study of cultural types so radically different as to exclude all possibility of conceptual ethnocentrism, and with luck, to spring open a few locks. . . .

One further remark: in the *Essai* of 1972, a certain grammatical formalism led me to reject the notion of "genres." To fill this void, I elaborated a typology of medieval texts founded on their modes of production and communication. I do not repent of this endeavor, though it errs by excessive systematization. It is indisputable that the concept of "genres," inasmuch as it results from a late and, I think, mistaken interpretation of Aristotle, is of no use to medievalists. Even more: it carries with it the seed of serious errors, in the definition and grouping of texts as well as in their comprehension. One could list all the untruths which, for this one reason, pepper the best studies published around 1950, and many of the same falsehoods still contaminate the manuals and books of popularization. For example, the idea that such and such a "genre" is destined, specifically for such and such a social class (the *fabliau*, the farce, are "addressed to the people," etc.); whence the untenable oppositions between "courtly poetry" and "bourgeois literature.". . . No one nowadays can seriously maintain these taxonomies.

It is nonetheless true that any account of history, in order to overcome the danger of dispersion into the multiplicity of the concrete, demands the intervention of criteria for grouping objects together, and of such criteria as may permit us, at least partially, to grasp the historicity of each text. The rare literary men or practitioners who, in the thirteenth century, managed to see this problem had the idea of a final purpose inherent in certain linguistic forms. Thus, from Ramon Vidal to Brunetto Latini and Dante, a critical tradition emerges, too sketchy, of course, to answer the questions we are posing today.

In the perspective that I mapped out above (having erased from our memories any tendencies to classicize), would it not be necessary rather to admit that there really are certain classes, even classes of classes, which together constitute (perhaps in an unsystematic but empirically effective way) a mediating function between the social infrastructure and the ideological superstructures? A regulating mechanism with the purpose of harmonizing the diverse experiences through which the contingent universe is apprehended? That is a conception held today by a number of German critics and medievalists: the "genres" (if one insists on keeping this old word while desubstantializing its content) in the functional order of history indicate something like a textual projection of the social institution. Basically, they signify an "orientation of expectations," as Jauss puts it, and designate the loci of collective semiosis.[33] We touch here on one of the nerve centers of our discipline.

§§§§·

The Romantic Heritage

The nature and urgency of the problems I am trying to enunciate (in very sketchy terms, I know) relate to our uncomfortable situation as medievalist-readers, trapped and at risk of being run over by several lanes of traffic at the crossroads where the last twenty-five years of criticism meet the growing technicalization of the human sciences and the actual history of our discipline.

Several times so far I have alluded to the latter. We need to retrace its main lines, if only to scratch away some of the "varnish of false interpretations laid down in the course of centuries," which, as Adorno wrote, encloses the work in the sphere of tradition.[34]

The fact that medieval studies were initially a manifestation of romanticism (I will inquire into neither the cause nor the effect of this fact) meant that a few presuppositions, whose vigor is noticeable in some places even today, were profoundly inscribed in the doctrine of nineteenth-century medievalists. I will designate four of them schematically.

The first emerges, on the level of critical discourse, in the notion of "origin," whatever may be the word that conveys it. The fascination with a detemporalized past willy-nilly drives historians (and even anthropologists, like Frazer) to accumulate an immense knowledge cut off from any living interest: extracted from the very instant in which research operates, this knowledge serves as the material from which to reconstruct a universe so distant and so insubstantial that it can be designated only by an empty generic term, our "Middle Ages" or "the primitive world." Mythic times, whose image makes reference to some archetypal purity, never clearly conceptualized, an inaccessible background upon which are floating vague pretextual convictions. In the beginning were the Good and the Beautiful, which have deteriorated over time. Here one would cite as example the first research on the epic and, more generally, an evolutionist vision of the history of texts. Resting on faith in a materially uninterrupted continuity and on spontaneous repugnance to the idea of polygenesis, this vision, like that of the first paleontologists, reduced science to the collation of remains and to the establishment of genealogies.

The reaction that has been manifested for a long time now against such monumentalizations remains hampered at times by the debris of that mythology, the idea of an original source, the idea of the value of a past without distance, directly comparable to the world of today—or rather of the day before yesterday, because, in fact, the ossification of imaginative and thought structures in nineteenth-century academic milieus often meant that, in 1930, 1940, or even 1950, the real point of reference was located in bourgeois society of 1850 or 1880![35]

In a complementary and more explicit way, purity resides in the eye of the reader, an eye treated beforehand with the wash of an erudition possessing the truth. Each person is said to have the natural gift of perceiving in a text the immediacy of a "testimonial." This is the facile way of justifying a privilege that camouflaged a servitude, a self-identification that reduces research to the quest for some "authenticity"—whether one takes this term in its most conventional philological meaning or as the absence, within the text, of unassimilable resistances and difficulties. What was thus too often glossed over even by the greatest of my mentors is a conflict that I myself would place at the center of our practice, a conflict that comes, as I have tirelessly repeated, from the congruence of a necessity and an uncertainty. A necessity to mark my nonidentity with my object in order to uphold the status of history, but an uncertainty as to the effects of the culture I bring to my reading of these texts, unearthed in the archeological layers of another world. Therefore, what killed the myth of "our origins," "the origin of," was no less a thing than the historicity of temporal distances.

A second romantic presupposition seems to me to be a displacement of the ancient idea of utopia. The temptation to which many medievalists succumbed, and still succumb (including Curtius, around 1950, on another level), was to dissimulate the gaps, not in their documentation, but in that mantle full of holes, history itself; to take some plaster kneaded with their ideology and patch those gaps potentially threatening to their own (good) conscience. Thus, recognizing the fundamentally hybrid quality of medieval civilization, they either blamed it on a pure and simple antinomy between so-called popular and learned, feudal and bourgeois cultures, relating to one or the other the simultaneous or successive manifestations of the discourse of that time; or they repudiated any dualist view and identified that civilization with an image of an *Ordo* conceived in neo-Thomist terms, furnishing all too easily some universal principle of interpretation, such as a symbol, figural allegory, or the edifice of Catholic dogmatism.

Today we have become skeptical of these well-ordered dreams, these nostalgias for epochs full of meaning, enclosed within themselves. Those Middle Ages never existed. What promoted them to the status of a mythical figure was not so much a doctrine as a mentality prevalent among the Fathers of medievalism. They had been marked by the upheavals of the first industrial revolution, in which, by compensation and reaction, the productions of the mind tended to take an intimist, autonomous, private direction, the self-defense of the isolated individual consoled by the privileges of his "culture" in the heart of the world's vulgarity.

A third presupposition: the intransitive character of the "literary" work. Posited a priori by most critics for a century and a half, it took effect among medievalists late, and in a very uneven way, in Bédier's time and under his influence.[36]

A fourth, intimately linked with the preceding: the notion of masterpiece, of little use and perhaps detrimental in medieval studies, in that it implies a sophistic and circular reasoning: a certain text constituted a factor in the grandeur of a certain era, an eminent manifestation of its "genius," without which that era would not have been what it was.

It is not a matter of denying qualitative differences, but rather of doubting our capacity to appreciate them. No one will deny that *The Divine Comedy* is more important to humanity than the *Chanson d'Aspremont*. But in what way and why? Perhaps, in the course of history, we must distinguish certain moments of cultural cohesion when the human group speaks the awareness it has of its identity, simultaneously and equally fully by all the body's means: the dance, the play of colors, the voice, writing, so that each of these registers takes only one part (necessarily fragmentary) in this concert; and other moments when the sum of human discourses is emblematically concentrated in a single register, or even in a small number of individual "works"—let's say the *Lancelot* by Chrétien de Troyes in the midst of the first crumblings of the feudal world, the *Quête du Graal* in a world shaken by the triumph of the first rationalisms. . . . Even these examples betray my hesitation. At the least, if one supposed some validity in this hypothetical typology, one would see the Middle Ages slipping more and more rapidly, between the eleventh and sixteenth centuries, from the first to the second cultural moment.

From the point of view of our own historicity, one can maintain with Jauss that the masterpiece manifests itself in the perspective of the past, in the guise of an unexpected and admirable change in the horizon of consideration. Something like a surplus of the word makes itself heard; a surplus of meaning demands to be perceived; it is irreducible to the significance of the traditional model. Whence a plenitude, impossible to define as such, but in general empirically proven by the ulterior history of produced interpretations.

From the point of view of the historicity of the object, the situation is even more obscure. The "masterpiece" is like the "great man" in traditional historiography. To confine our studies to the "museum without walls" gradually constructed by our predecessors is to condemn them forever to that idealist aesthetic according to which "great art" is always immediately present. But the history of manuscript traditions, of adaptations and translations, of glosses, of late introductions or continuations added to a previous text, of all those common medieval practices, sometimes reveals such differences between twelfth- and thirteenth-century readers and twentieth-century ones in the reception, comprehension, and appreciation of texts that any transfer of judgment seems problematic.[37]

Therefore, within its own order, no knowledge could possibly define the masterpiece: it is a historically radical impossibility. Who, however, and in the name of what prohibition, will ever prevent us from thinking, from saying, of a certain text, "this masterpiece"? The source of all these ambiguities lies in the fact that when we pronounce this phrase, we situate ourselves in the order of pleasure, and of pleasure alone.

§ Positive Negative

This heavy and complex romantic heritage still weighs on us. What has been acquired since then has overloaded and altered it, not replaced it. Perhaps it is today in the German hermeneutic, under Gadamer's influence, that its most fertile elements have been preserved, to engender lively continuations. Elsewhere the results are more dubious.

The first impetus of European romanticism became middle-class, cross-bred with positivism, and finally enmired itself, late in the century, in various nationalisms and, less openly, in social conservatism. Scientism and naive historicism were added to this, among scholars who were then clearing the medieval terrain, along with a new humanism fundamentally mistrustful of the procedures of art.

Impugning a discourse which was anarchic in their eyes and which generated combinations ever more unexpected as the century passed by, these men appealed to the sole authority of assured idioms, with a guaranteed identity, whose model at that time was furnished by scientific argumentation. Whence the systems of repression K. Stierle speaks about, after Foucault: an intention of truth, a "tabouisation" of the irrational, an impersonalization of the word—and, we would add with Barthes, a hidden will to power. This order of discourse tended to impose on studies of a historical nature the "Euclidean" model elaborated by Aristotle and founded on a closed series of axioms, primary concepts, and derived propositions. The scientific enterprise consisted in the elaboration of a dictionary, the fabrication of a machine to make a given signifier coincide in an unequivocal way with a given signified—so that everything in the world becomes readable and appropriable. Philological discourse identified itself with what J. Bellemin-Noël calls "the rhetoric of the systemized review"; it rejected with abomination, crossed out in its own writing, anything that might permit the reader to participate in the progression, the chances, the possible illegitimacy of a piece of research.

It was a far cry from the grand synthesis dreamed by Vico a century before. Ancient, noble Philologia was reduced to an inventory of "objective facts," banishing interpretation to a place within the auxiliary sciences: the "explication de texte" to which rightly or wrongly we attach the name of Lanson.[38]

For a long time no one expressed doubts on these points. The socio-historical milieu was reflected in the mirror-text; there was no mystery there. "Facts" were all that existed. The romantic myth of continuity, appropriated but displaced, was applied henceforth to the fabric of those facts, defining the languages and nations whose essential and permanent character it was important to demonstrate after 1848 and, even more so, in France and Germany after 1870. This attitude, held by almost all medievalists up until the Second World War, implied a complete misunderstanding of the intercultural relationship that places us in opposition to our object, a relationship which, as we have seen, carries the necessity of posing an epistemological question before taking up any discussion about methods. The Fathers of medieval studies, on the whole, set aside this question. That is why they did not, at any time, attempt to extract a theory from their own practice.

The greatest among them possessed immense knowledge, of which we are still the beneficiaries; but they never questioned the ideological and philosophical implications of their way of working: that is, by collecting information and transmitting it to their disciples and readers. Whence the unquestioning tenacity with which they attached themselves to contingent criteria, posed as absolutes: unity, organicity, and others. These criteria determined an argumentation which was analogical in type but which thought of itself as deductive.

The romantic myth of the origin, in its turn, became commonplace. In the now distant time when I was initiated into these studies, the search for "sources" was the dominant preoccupation: the troubadours were "explained" by Ovid or by Ibn Hazm, if not by the Goliards; the *chansons de geste* by the hypothetical cantilenas or by the *Waltharius*. There was Jean Marx, good-natured and pompous in his handsome apartment across from the nave of Notre Dame, and William Nitze, ticking off middle western platitudes with the elegance of a lord. They were cataloguing, without always agreeing, the "Breton themes" presumed to have come from far-off mythologies, while virtually ignoring their real narrative function. Correspondences were promoted to the status of causes, which meant ascribing to an individual will those convergences whose only meaning is collective. The "search for sources," giving voice to a silence, articulates a possibility, nothing more. Indispensable, and in itself without interest, it does nothing but mark its place in a process that redistributes historical space; it is related to a different functioning, another discourse, for which it has not the power to substitute itself. Far from constituting a referent for historical discourse, it reified a referential illusion. As a reincarnation of the old principle of authority, the explanation by means of sources supposed all questions related to transmission and reception of discourses to be resolved. As for the texts themselves, they were reduced to documents; anything else was considered self-evident. In 1943, in my thesis, I was already becoming vaguely aware of these misapprehensions and trying clumsily to avoid them: perhaps at that time I had already understood that history, while explaining nothing, has the task of making things explicit.

§ Literary History?

We were living in the autocratic reign of "literary history," a name and a concept that had, with simplicity and simplification, been extended to cover virtually everything written at a particular moment in time. Exhuming and reconstituting the "facts," it ordered them with a discourse that was in itself difficult to prove wrong, because the only criticism to which it lay open concerned its content, the archival value of the documents underlying the arguments. It was metonymic discourse, proceeding by proximities through successive descriptions, according to unexamined basic options: the possibility of identifying these "facts"[39] and the links between them; the functionality of external causes, the singularity of what is "true," whence the easy flow back and forth from the text to the author, from the writing to episodes of life, a concretization of the functional. In this way, "literary history," closely linked with the dominant ideology, was concealing the pertinence of social and biographical factors supposed to account for the text, by its very research into those facts.

E. Hicks has recently surveyed successive interpretations of the famous "Quarrel of the *Roman de la Rose*," an episode in Parisian literary life of around 1400. From 1856 to 1972 we witness the recombination of a few pieces of information, widely known since the 1880s, recycled in each generation within the narrow circle of received ideas, carried from thesis to manual and then into new theses by means of a kind of cancerization in the system. A minuscule example. We could cite hundreds of others. E. Köhler in 1976 made the same sort of attack on troubadour studies; P. von Moos in 1974 had submitted to pitiless examination the long series of books devoted, in the course of three centuries, to Abelard and Héloïse.

In the absence of a theory, a tendency originating in some distant Hegelianism served as organizing principle for these fragmented realities: the notion of "epoch" was clothed in epistemological dignity; it evoked the Spirit in its objectivity, and subsumed pell-mell into a factitious unity the most heterogeneous elements: the need to organize history's chaotic waves into harmonious and closed representations, representations constituted on the basis of a few facts (a few texts) pronounced significant to the detriment of others. But facts, as we know today, organize themselves in series whose diachronic parameters differ, so that it is their disjunctures and reciprocal shifts, rather than their convergences, that make up our vision of history: the only true problem that remains is to define the mutual articulation of certain of these series, taking account of the level on which their evolution operates and of the rhythm that characterizes this evolution.[40]

A doctrinaire and falsely systematic tendency hardened this somewhat amorphous body of habits and doctrines. Philology, even reduced to its grammatical aspect, served as a slogan and ultimate justification. Jauss, after Robert Guiette, analyzed its dogmas.[41] Two dominant traits emerge: the reduction of all signification (supposedly hidden behind the text) to unicity, whence a refusal of what was ambiguous, plural, or implied; on the part of the philologist, a radical egocentrism taking as a principle the fact that literature had been made for him. It took the depth of spirit and the artistic sense of a Bédier, an Auerbach, a Curtius, to break the circle of tautologies on this point.

These habits of thought, distributed very unevenly according to the temperament and training of researchers, schools, and centers, maintained an ensemble of more or less explicit ideological criteria linked to what was called "humanistic discourse."[42] It was the discourse of a learned stage in whose wings the actors hurled insults at each other about "assured facts," "risky hypotheses," "corrupted versions," and "authentic texts," in a conflict that was all the more acute because it was never called by its true name: no one put his cards on the table. Everyone laid claim to that absence of point of view which allowed an illusory neutrality of values; then, withdrawn into the bookish tranquillity of the study, one restored oneself in a slow, meticulous labor of establishing and classifying index cards whose effect was to remove the drama from life, death, and the destiny of men.

Our medievalists in the late nineteenth century, and still in the early twentieth, were in fact subscribing, all over Europe, to a debilitated aesthetic, implying an unshaken faith in the transparency of language as well as a taste for "the great commonplaces that move us" and for the "sincerity" that characterizes them: most of these values eluded classification on index cards, making the task all the easier. Gaston Paris, sensitive soul that he was, swore that he did not have to concern himself with "the beauties of poetry," because they are not to be taught, but felt!

Whence their summary verdicts: they condemned as garbled any opacity in discourse (unless it was attributable to some copyist's error!); they praised for its "humanity" any utterance which, often taken out of context, seemed interpretable in terms of an avowal or a reference to external nature, transcendant to the words whose supposed function was to manifest it. Among the sociocultural determinisms governing this procedure, one that weighed heavily for generations (especially with French medievalists) was that prejudice according to which "cultural" history, moving either backward or forward in time, was clarified on the basis of a central epistemic moment, identified with "classicism" (from Descartes to the Encyclopedists) in relation to which any opposition could be defined. Thus entrenched, the historiography of medieval texts came down to an amiable intellectual tourism, similar to the one that reveals to ladies with cameras the discrete charm of the Yucatán Indians.

To be sure, the specialized medievalist, saved by his erudition, thereby evades wrongheaded simplifications more easily than ordinary mortals; but at a less precise level of consciousness his judgment nonetheless is too often prefabricated: for him, the permanent identity of the linguistic, poetic, and textual facts that he studies flow eternally from the Grand Model: the sixteenth, seventeenth, and eighteenth centuries, which were, in many respects only a brief regressive episode in Western history. "Middle Ages," an expression created around 1500, designates (not without condescension) the long, ever so laborious preliminary phase of a movement destined to blossom in a *Renaissance*. And the closer the research area is to the emblematic term of this centenary turning point, the more pronounced are the distortions.

Thus the fascinating fifteenth century appears, in the bibliography of "medieval literature," as a sort of no man's land of uncertain attribution in which one world is said to be coming apart, another said to be emerging, leaving the philologist without criteria. The official teaching of medieval literature is still today, especially in France, partly the victim of this false perspective.

True, sometimes, even in moments of triumphant positivism, a work animated by some potent personality succeeded in making a clear voice heard in the midst of general impotence: an effect of personal genius, capable of grasping at its critical point such and such a piece of the real, despite a sterilizing system that was in no way called into question. Thus, in our century Jean Frappier showed perfect intellectual honesty and extensive knowledge, and also a proper measurement of his own space (after the posings of Gustave Cohen, that enthusiastic and mediocre popularizer). Frappier's qualities had an exemplary value for people of my age and at the same time suggested all that remained to be done. Similarly, in Rome there was Angelo Monteverdi, a man of princely bearing and sometimes d'Annunzian discourse; still, many parts of his works gave me, around 1950 or '60, the point of departure for a reflection on causes.

Men of this calibre have enabled "the history of medieval literature" not only to survive but also, recently, to begin to reconstitute itself on the basis of different premises: first in Germany, where Werner Krauss, in 1959, broached the problematics of double historicity, and where, in the 1970s, Jauss integrated with his aesthetics of reception a dialectic of the literary time span inspired by Russian formalism. Since then, in Italy, in France, from one center to the next we have seen attempts at a new systematization. This was what I meant to accomplish, in a very limited area, with my book on the Rhétoriqueurs.

§ The Insular Text

This movement of ideas attempts to transcend not only conventional literary history, but also the aftereffects (fairly limited, really, in medieval studies) of a formalism originating in Saussure and Hjelmslev.

We know how rapidly the twentieth century, especially after the First World War, eroded previous scientific traditions. Starting before 1900, the bourgeois codes of signification had been periodically shaken by the blows of an artistic avant-garde, despised in scholarly circles but nonetheless functioning to favor a return to the subjective;[43] the work of Joseph Bédier illustrates its effects. In the course of the 1920s new methods emerged, modes of knowledge manifesting a tendency to reject the obsession with history: structuralism, Freudian psychoanalysis. After the Second World War, this tendency seemed momentarily to triumph absolutely: medievalists of my generation lived this experience in the 1950s. Several of us were attracted by the diffuse prestige of the Saussurian school, and then of the Copenhagen linguists. For me, the first intermediary was Benvenuto Terracini, one of the mentors for whom I still hold the highest admiration. Having become concerned with rigorous formal descriptions, each of us set off in quest of structures whose functional analysis would replace the old ways of aleatory interpretation: our predecessor Reto Bezzola, followed by a group of remarkable disciples, opened the way, around 1947, in his Zurich chair; in Germany, the work of W. Kellermann took a similar path; that of Silvio D. Avalle in Italy and, in France, in a way that avoided a complete break with history, the early research of Daniel Poirion, no less than the various essays of Pierre Guiraud.

Our common tendency, above and beyond our divergences, was a turning back upon the text itself, the text made sacred: the second dialectical term (thus it seems now, at a distance of these few years) of an antinomic process whose end may today be approaching.

The very conditions of our studies predestined us, as it then seemed to me, to this ascesis. The frequency of anonymous texts, the uncertainty of dating, had always imposed narrow limits on the application of Lansonian methods. The fifteenth century, from this point of view, was tending toward the modern era: hence the biographical nature of almost everything published on Villon or the Grands Rhétoriqueurs. It would be better, I thought, as did a number of my colleagues, in order to purify the air of the laboratory and give more meaning to the experiment, to go back in time as far as an era (from the ninth to the twelfth century) in which there remained no means of identifying the activity of a subject except the product itself: the text, isolated, drowned in a history with vague outlines, traced in dotted lines so discontinuous that a problem arose at each one of their intersections. A problem that could only be enunciated in the contradictory terms of inertia and active re-production. That is what I attempted in my little book *Langue et techniques poétiques à l'époque romane*, written in 1961, while in journals like *Vox romanica* in Switzerland, *Cultura neolatina* in Italy, in several colloquia and congresses, there began a reevaluation of the problems surrounding the formation of the oldest romance cultures.

However, for fifteen years we had already been quietly overtaken, by that great man Robert Guiette, scholar and poet, friend, since the twenties, of Cendrars, Max Jacob, Michaux, and who died without fanfare in 1976. It was around 1960 that his message reached me, and I gauged its importance by what Roger Dragonetti had drawn from it, in what to me was the first convincing book on the poetry of *fine amour*. It took some time to assimilate this neostructuralism, nourished by the aesthetics of music, which immediately implicated in a reading, along with the reader himself, his psychic and moral history, categorically rejecting the prejudice of the univocality of texts.

We were still digesting this contribution when in 1967 Julia Kristeva reopened the whole discussion of history (on another level and, I must admit, in less amiable language) by importing to France, apropos of a fifteenth-century text, the notion of an ideologeme. However, around here and, to a lesser degree, in Germany, Italy, and the United States, people had not yet stopped assimilating the recently discovered Russian or Prague formalism: the idea of literarity, made commonplace, polarized vast and sometimes tumultuous sectors of research. My task, I imagined, would be to sketch a definition of medieval literarity, a contradictory enterprise, because it implied the abandonment, and at the same time the reappropriation, of the "nonliterary" as history. I used the idea of "tradition" to make this transition and, by an expositional artifice, affected a basic skepticism as to the pertinence of external references for the comprehension of texts as such.

It was in this context that, between 1968 and '71, I wrote my *Essai de poétique médiévale*, in which today I can discern a double lack of perspective. Literarity, a modern concept, cannot, without begging the question, found an archeology. As for the reaction against documentary historicism, an admissible tactic but one without absolute value, it cannot found a strategy. And at the very moment when I was joyfully devoting myself to this work, it was becoming evident, beyond the walls of my study, that, on account of a shift that had taken place in the deep levels of our civilization, the disciplines given to studying works of art or literary texts were beginning, with the aid of Marx and Freud, to harbor mistrust toward the very materials of these works, toward the language manifested in these texts, refusing to accept it as existing in nature. Would everything have to be redone, after the *Entkünstung der Kunst*, as Adorno called it?

Maybe not. The time was past when medievalists marched in step, in impeccable rows, in front of the same barracks. More and more, paths diverged. From the time, before 1940, when, with a pioneer's serene contempt for decorum, Albert Pauphilet had proposed his allegorical interpretation of the *Quête du Graal*, that type of speculation had found in Anglo-Saxon countries, especially the United States, favorable soil and eminent practitioners, apparently under the influence of "new criticism" and its habit of the "close reading": C. S. Lewis, D. W. Robertson, and, more recently, John Fleming. R. Kirckpatrick recently submitted to close examination the implications of their reading of Dante.[44] In Europe, from the mid-1960s on, a reevaluation of allegory as a mode of signification and rule of reading had greater interest for the likes of Guiette, Jauss, Poirion, Marc-René Jung, myself, and, from a more exegetical standpoint, Jean Pépin and Fathers de Lubac and Chenu.

Already several propositions may be put forth: contrary to a widespread opinion, the "literature of the Middle Ages" is only rarely "symbolic." What to us (as another result of romanticism) seems a symbol, an object productive of a meaning that is other and, in principle, inexhaustible, functioned for the medieval man rather as an enigma, catering to his taste for the obscure, the ambiguous, the suspenseful; but its solution was scarcely more important than winning a game with no stakes.[45] Allegory, however, constituted a procedure of rationalization, of logical reduction of the visual by explicit reference to a system of Resemblances—whose continuous disintegration from the thirteenth to the sixteenth century I believe I have demonstrated. Disintegrated or not, it referred to one or to several codes, whose nature and mutual relations are gradually brought to light. Yet there remains a lot of underbrush to clear in this *selva oscura*, research and reconstitution of the codes in

54

question. This means abandoning pure and simple descriptions and having recourse to at least a few principles of contemporary semiotics, thereby bringing about what must be brought about: a confrontation between a target text and our own historicity, undeniable and manifested by the very nature of the effort it costs us to produce a meaning that may explain the one which, for other readers, was doubtless intuitively and globally understood as real.

But the real is historical; the obvious is obvious in only one time. What for us constitutes reality did not necessarily do so in the twelfth century—and I am not alluding here only to technical and scientific evolution. Our critical reading of medieval allegory will therefore, once again, consist of a reaction, in that an interpreter implies both a translator and a living voice. To interpret, to explain, to make explicit this or that figure is to make it yield (after our erudition has dusted it off) a meaning that might be our own. Isn't this the very operation which learned men of the Middle Ages practiced on antique texts (without being able to measure their scope very well)? They were trying to surmount a cultural distance (of which they were not much aware) and also to appropriate a heritage.

This was how, in medieval studies, orthodox structuralism was barely established before it was overthrown. Refracting the complex mass of the real through a set of terms that fragments it, structuralist models, like semiotic models, some of which have emerged from them, were organizing for a time our apprehension of the natural world; they were releasing new energy and introducing a new dimension into our problematics. But this did not happen without a certain theoretical hardening, a step backward from practice, a certain contempt for the concrete. In its preliminary and instrumental phase (in a pluralist perspective), structural analysis sets up, at a distance, a reading of what is said without being said. It is legitimate and productive only when a scale of intelligibility intervenes between the events so delimited, allowing us to reestablish a continuous relationship: the claim of history. Walter Benjamin was already proclaiming this in the thirties, discerning in the structuralist process a weakening of the conscience, which, by the way, seemed to pertain to the West and be less apparent among members of the Russian and Prague school, who concerned themselves with describing the dynamism of the system rather than its inner workings.

It's useless to insist. We could cover whole library shelves with the records of this trial. In the course of the seventies the warnings proliferated, denouncing a series of presuppositions less and less tolerable in the concrete world we live in: the existence of a closed linguistic universe; the defining of sign systems independently of their production and reception; the reification of structures; the reduction of communication to a combinatory play of formal logic; the totalization of analytical givens.[46]

Structuralist discourse, in its period of triumph, lay in the realm of yes or no. It did not recognize what was intense, shifting, fluid. It supposed a solid, devoid of energy, unsuited to integrating into its system that violence which the text must have in order to be grasped, and which we must have in order to feel it. What is important today lies, not in the order of structures, but in the order of the underlying processes that maintain them. If it has become hard to ignore notions of structure and sign, it has become still harder not to think of dispersion, loss, and hope.

§ Types of Writing

Thus, over time, across these modes and occasional storms, my companions and I have not ceased "doing history"; by that I mean we have attempted to produce a model of intelligibility that includes ourselves: less by a reduction to the event, which is, perhaps, the text, than by construction of givens that are repetitive, regular, and comparable (without claiming either exhaustiveness or mathematical precision); one of these givens would implicate us personally. However, in the period around 1960 and 1965, we were encountering a new friend, one who had little apparent interest in our problems but without whom I felt we would go no further. I am speaking of Roland Barthes, and, on the horizon, those who had already begun to follow him.

Writing, text, history: more than in the concepts which refer to them, it was as processes of signification at work in the elements of the corpus that we have to define them, dismantle them; to effect an opening in what closes our discourse by its very finitude, to bring the "finished" product back to its unfinished and infinite production, to deconstruct a given object, conceived hypothetically as a montage. A montage of the relationships which com-pose it and which it necessarily supposes. But these relationships are formed in mobile configurations, whose identity becomes apprehensible only at a more general and common level—in the case of the Middle Ages, on the level of "tradition." Yet one must not be duped by the implications of this term: tradition is conveyed not so much by systems as by modes of signification, and the subject who articulates these modes remains outside the frame, a blank point on the wall, placing in focus this text which is other than that subject.

Even then, we had to maintain distinctions and not unthinkingly assimilate old texts whose mode of social functioning we barely knew.

I adopted, as a convenient hypothesis, a distinction suggested by Barthes, clarified by others, opposing, in relation to modern centuries, two types of writing corresponding to two signifying practices: one, founded on signification, expression, representation; the other on production and on the self-representation of production. On the one hand, the texts of "modernity"; on the other, all the rest. The ensemble of critical instruments perfected in the last twenty years refer especially, if not exclusively, to the former, to those books manifesting in an obvious way the self-proclaimed practice of writing, whence a semantic availability, as opposed to the plenitude of the "classic" book, whose polysemy is limited and stems at best from a false transparency. To be sure, it would be impossible to invoke in this context an unbridgeable gap between two firmly established types. Both one and the other seem (on first look) to coexist in the medieval corpus; and if at times perhaps one predominates, it never entirely displaces the other. Why not begin with the more "modern" in order to illuminate the more "classic," without thereby reducing the one to the other, since the "modern" manifests only what the "classic" represses and since in any case the pre-text is implied in the "tradition"?

I myself for years have been pointing out, in works from the Carolingian *carmina figurata* to the Grands Rhétoriqueurs, traces of a "writing" that eludes its own order and ideology by the sole means of its inscription. Bit by bit, it appeared to me that for those texts, neither the author's intention (supposing that it can be established) nor the immediate perceptibility of semantic traits constitutes a sufficient, or even valid, criterion for reading. Whence a general suspicion: would this not in itself be a revealing phenomenon and suggest in an early stage a mode of approach, certainly approximate but not aberrant, applicable to all the writings left to us by that great civilization? Romances and poems in which we will presume that no one is offering himself to be read, in which the author has completely "depersonalized" himself in the production of his text: a characteristic which, if one admits it, marks in a global way the difference between the "Middle Ages" and what immediately followed it.

The work, subsequently called "open," according to Umberto Eco's formulation, condemns the logocentrism which until recently characterized the Western traditions. Here is a reemergence of the subject, masked, protean: the text that functions in the heart of a cluster of social determinations.

For some (especially east of the Rhine) the reality of writing comes from a continuous exchange between the production and consumption of the texts; for many French critics, it is located rather in the play of mirrors and the disparities that constitute this very production. But, in dissimilar programmatic guises, in the midst of this outburst of doctrines and these diffuse efforts, one may discern, in medieval studies, certain things converging, strategically if not methodologically: it is not impossible to imagine that in the distant future we will all meet at the same point—a great gathering of energies contributing actively to the birth of a new civilization: a gathering which I will have dreamed about during my lifetime but in which I will probably not be able to participate. Or, perhaps, "medieval literature," definitively devalorized, will have fallen into oblivion.

At times we seek in the narrow margins of the erudite tradition, by attentively examining contextual and extratextual factors, the plausible model of a textual intention: for example, in Nancy

Freeman Regalado's book on Rutebeuf and, in part, my own book on the Rhétoriqueurs. At times we venture into the literal deciphment of the text's ruses, of the historically significant obverse of its syntax: for example, in Evelyn Birge-Vitz's study of Villon or in Marie-Louise Ollier's series of articles on the twelfth-century verse romance. From there one may easily move to a psychoanalytic reading, of which Charles Méla has recently furnished examples that are at once debatable and passionately innovative. Certain areas more than others have inspired this kind of effort: today the romance, yesterday the *chanson de geste*.[47]

I recognize in all this work both the laying aside, or transcending, of Saussuro-Hjelmslevian semiology (itself broken down into semiotics of communication and semiotics of meaning) and a progressive reorientation of the gaze onto history conceived as the existing relationship between the text and ourselves. Thus it is as if some obscure and delicious determinism were leading us back, by a spiral stairway, to the basic medieval position, from which the text interprets itself dramatically rather than logically. Similarly, as Eugene Vance says, a musician "interprets" a sonata better by performing it than by analyzing it.

A thing is mediated by language or it isn't. But was "literature" something medieval? According to Roland Barthes's formulation, is literature not the fruit of some wish other than a refusal to take part in the absence of parallelism between the real and what man can say about the real?[48] Here the real is the physical existence of those marks that constitute the text. That is what makes the meaning: producer, production, and product, never fixed, but nonetheless the undeniable and ultimate basis of our discourses.

§ Tradition and *Mouvance*

So many blind spots and irretrievable zones still remain.[49] I have already spoken of the excessive optimism with which, not long ago, I tried to incorporate even what was inaccessible into the notion of tradition, stripped of teleological implications, conceived as the place where the texts' historicity is inscribed. By that

I hoped to grasp, at a level of abstraction just high enough, an object that is indefinable a priori. Though I would not altogether reject that idea today, I would modulate it, seeking in tradition not so much a "competence" in the generativist sense as a network of relationships. And these, then, should be evoked in terms sufficiently nuanced to allow for their instability, their inherent need for an incessant reevaluation and for an opening onto the unexpected. Whatever may in fact be the force of a discursive or poetic tradition, and in spite of what is self-determined in this tradition, one could never deny that mutations take place here and there within it under the impact of extratextual factors; in particular, in any culture of a "traditional" type (in the anthropologists' sense), discourses are generally enunciated *in presentia:* whence the basic "theatricality" of any medieval poetic text, whose apparent inertia, stemming from its being written down, is only a mask imposed upon it.

I suggested that a dotted line separated the symbol from the type, and from the latter, the myth or the emblem; one inflection of the voice, one gestural allusion (and what do we know about that sort of code?) or one element of décor sufficed to eliminate it.[50] This subversion, possible at any moment, blurs the contours of "tradition" and allows a new reading even today.

All that remains, in fact, within the range of our gaze, after an often arid investigation, is the critical moment at which the appropriation, by the medieval text, of a preexistent element, is manifested in a deviance or a denial—or, rather, in deviant or denying tendencies, because in this context any idea of a "poetic revolution" would be inapplicable. The shifts, the twists, and even a certain appetite for rupture never attempted, before the fifteenth or sixteenth century, to block the system. The system nonetheless was unfailingly affected, but to what extent? Shouldn't a probability of error be integrated into our reading?

Another impossibility: distance in time and cultures conceals the individual subject from us: at best a few snatches of anecdotal information mask our ignorance. We can only conceive the individual on the basis of our own historicity, in relation to the conscious boundaries within whose limits we live and move. Beyond that stretches a vast, fluid space, with vaguely cosmic coordinates, resistant to extrapolations by analogy. Thus I will have to presume, not an "author," but a locus for the organizations of forms, a group surrounding the speaker and posited, in relation to him, in a hypostatic position, implying or not implying a common will. But can one, in this situation, proclaim the "death of the subject," that false novelty that was so much talked about a few years ago? There remains on our pages, at the least, a grammatical figure, ambiguous but all the more impossible to elude, because the "I," in medieval theatricality, could not fail to imply the listener and his need for individuation.[51]

Finally, I refer to the idea of the *mouvance* of texts, which I proposed in my *Essai* and which several of my colleagues have adopted for themselves. But, there too, it is possible that I generalized too freely. Wouldn't it be by an attentive examination of the facts of *mouvance* proper to *each* "work" that we would arrive at what constitutes the key to this ensemble of problems: the manner in which medieval texts confronted the "horizon of expectations" of people in their own time? But even supposing such a task feasible on the information level, does not posing the question (which we must do) imply our transcending of the notion of code, our apparent ideological elimination of ideology, and our use of a sort of metasemiosis in the perpetual flight of interpretants? The recipient of the text has a role, inscribed in the text: reception and interpretation, concretization and reelaboration cannot be dissociated—still less in oral performance than in written transmission. The text aims to intoxicate the one who receives it, even when it has to invent him. However, Robert Guiette, for his part, said that medieval poetry is conceived from the point of view of its maker, not of its listener, and that its end is to pour out the joy of an act. . . .

This only appears to be a contradiction. It was certainly in these double terms that people of the twelfth century understood their own poetry—if I can allow myself (as I believe I can) to apply to profane material what Bernard of Clairvaux wrote about the *Song of Songs*. "That which the poem sings only a humble veneration may teach us; only to feel it allows us to understand it. Therefore let those who can experience it recognize it; and let those who cannot burn with desire, not to know, but to feel. This is not so much a word from the lips as a leap of joy; a harmony of the intention more than of the voice. It is not, as it seems, on the outside that one hears it, nor in public places that it truly resounds: only those who sing it hear it, and those for whom it is sung."[52]

In such a reading, of course, nothing is ever an established fact. Each question I ask the object touches it, me, and the question itself. That is why the end of the process is by nature deferred; the result it seeks is contradictory, because it is supposed to be the abolition of the other and of the self. But, further, interpretation (contrary to the romantic prejudice) is not infinite. It has its limits and its rules, though they are unstable, incessantly to be revised: the limits associated with documentary verisimilitude, the rules stemming from our own intellectual disciplines. In any case, it will be able only to suggest, never to conclude: because for us there seems no longer to be a meaning, only interpretations. Philosophy has had its day. What remains is our myths as we recite them, our weariness of falsely reassuring rationalities, and our need for the imaginary rather than the intelligible.

§ The Irretrievable

The work of art is tautological, in the sense that it does not "express": it is. In the same way, poetry has never "declared" anything: poetry tries to capture something of the world which it confronts but from which it is separated by a fundamental insufficiency, though it may capture some far-off, fugitive gleams of it. Even thought is also a "tolerance of non-thought," in the words of Michel Deguy, an obscurity, irremediable but positive. Such propositions, when applied to medieval poetry, are true in a special way, even more historical than ontological, having to do with the appearance this civilization assumes in our eyes when seen at a distance of several centuries.

The Middle Ages, as I have said, were unaware of "literature." What's more, they did not, until very late, construct a notion comparable to ours of "poetry"—just as they never set up (as J. Jolivet, P. Vignaux, and others have shown) a "philosophy." Theology, certainly: *lectio divina;* but when the word "philosophy" appears in practice, it refers to the allegorical Hermes of Martianus Cappella, to the transmission of knowledge, and finally to alchemy. It designates not so much a doctrine or even a discourse as a path of action, this action itself, and its rule; it refers less to authors than to the empirical representatives of an artisanal tradition. It aims at a transmutation: here from base metals to gold, elsewhere from language to meaning.[53] But the one does not differ from the other any more than the "philosopher" engaged in his Great Work might have differed from the troubadour, the extractor of *fine amour* in the alembic of his song. Here I do not mean to express myself metaphorically: it is more than probably that the word *fine,* in this expression, was an alchemical term.

On the other hand, it is probably a metonymic relation by which, on a chain of verbal transmutations and "hermeticism" of meaning, one might integrate the effects of that generalized practice called, in its various forms, irony. My books have not been the only ones in the last twenty years to point out its omnipresence in medieval poetic discourse. I will not press this point.[54]

One might maintain, not too paradoxically, that every medieval poetic form (on whatever level one may define it) *tends* toward double meaning: and I don't mean the doubling deciphered by an allegoristic reading but, superimposing or complexifying its effects, a perpetual *sic et non,* yes and no, obverse/reverse. Every meaning, in the last analysis, would present itself as enigmatic, the enigma being resolved into simultaneous and contradictory propositions, one of which always more or less parodies the other. Peter Haidu bases one of the constants of romance on this figure, understood very broadly; as for me, I would scarcely hesitate to interpret the poetry of *fine amour* globally in this way, specifically because of its interferences with the contemporary tradition of the *detractiones amoris.*

Some have thought to see in these tendencies the impact of class conflict: an anecdotal explanation. I would be more inclined to wonder, with H. Gumbrecht, if, in its ensemble and general intention, medieval poetry in the vernacular does not present (very diffusely, but betraying its presence through irony) the character of what we would call a counterculture, which we know today to have found its form in the carnival, a form, paradoxically, institutionalized.[55]

Thus, at best, the abstract term of our studies could be the establishment of an organized network of "ideal types," of partially overlapping "models." This network would sketch, in more or less blurred strokes, in dotted lines, something like the geography of the utopian country where one would see the eventual meeting of the structural lines and energy currents found in our object, the fragment of history. Thus, we would enlarge our angle of vision and at the same time maintain the factor of uncertainty without which no further questions would ever be asked; without which, for lack of desire, no knowledge could ever be constituted.

§§§§§·

A Necessary Empiricism

That is the situation. Now it's up to us to speak, that is, to take up the word, to seize an object, invest it with discourse, and make it yield symbolic returns that are negotiable but subject to all the hazards of the stock exchange.

In the preceding I have put considerable emphasis on the complexity of the tasks confronting the critical reader of "medieval literature," obligated to practice a historical discourse, but on texts. This imperative, burdened as it is with numerous contradictions, poses a fundamental problem: is our practice theorizable?

The tools that facilitate its exercise are partly, if not mainly, conceptual in nature. The concepts themselves are subject to two types of utilization: dogmatic/systematic or heuristic/empiric, a distinction that could serve as a criterion for categorizing the methods now being elaborated, whose success will determine whether or not our studies have a future. My position (as the reader will already have guessed) tends to be somewhat in the margins, at some distance from these trends, in the more fluid zone of thought which I would call, if I can venture such a word, theoretico-empirical.

It is empirical primarily on account of the extent to which I implicate myself; the extent to which, in my discourse, I hear a voice I know to be my own, however altered, however foreign, because what is heard in it is my own problem, one that I may neither elude nor truly know. It is theoretical in the extent to which, according to Fredric Jameson, a "proto-political" value is attached to what I say: important to our common destiny in a sure, though unpredictable, way.

65

It is empirical also because not only do these old texts speak to me, each in its own voice; they also question me and solicit a response that will speak to each one of them. The allegory and emblematism underlying and dynamizing all medieval poetic discourse identify any "writing" with the gloss it is meant to elicit, the foreseeable explication of its meanings. The medieval text offers me its trust. Even when its literal word manifests a violence, it likes me; it expects my benevolence and my adherence to its mysteries. Everything it says to us is exemplary: what it tries to provoke in me is a *conversio*, a turning around by which the other side of appearances will appear. A multiform commonplace programs this intention into many an exordium: the text says, I give you a meaning; it is yours to discover, to "invent"—as they used to say of the *invention* of a saint's relics. The *Roman de la Rose* by Guillaume de Lorris illustrates this purpose in a remarkable way, but in doing so, that admirable text serves only to illuminate all the others. Our task, in each particular case, will consist of discovering in what words, along what lines, the text means to guide our steps.

The text exists only inasmuch as it is read. To know it is to read it; and reading is a practice, realizing the union of our thought with this thing it accepts, perhaps provisionally, as real. Thus, reading is, at least potentially, a dialogue; but in it two agents confront one another: I am in some way produced by this text, and in the same moment, as a reader, I construct it. A relationship of active solidarity rather than a mirror-effect; a solidarity promised rather than given, pleasurably felt at the end of the long preparatory work required by the traversing of two historical distances, going and coming back.[56]

The need for intelligibility arises nonetheless and requires that the reading transcend itself in some shifting and evolving synthesis. The end we seek is pragmatically double: in a primary but necessary way, it is to construct the "model" of this text, to "make the accidental essential," as Paul Klee put it. This duality is linked to the conditions governing our present learning, to the structure of our thought and our knowledge. It is a result of the very purpose of our attempt to know, in the epistemic situation of our culture.

Thus the medievalist's discourse will have two components, more tightly intertwined than that "history" which Croce used to distinguish from "chronicle." On the one hand, this discourse will represent a reality which was once concrete but which has ceased to be so; on the other, it has to elaborate the description conceptually, on pain of producing, possibly under a title patented by the Institution, some monstrous constructions that evoke the bric-a-brac of seekers after the philosopher's stone.

A poetics, writes Henri Meschonnic (in words that apply equally well to medieval poetics) has its own rigor, but no models.[57] Let's be clear on the meaning we should attribute to this last term. I would discard (thereby in the main confirming Meschonnic) any idea of a pure, mathematizable abstraction. I would also avoid concretizing the concept under the designation *Weltmodell* proposed by Jauss, referring to a more or less closed whole, not of representations, but of rules which, for us, function as rules for decoding, valid for the operations practiced by the one who constructs the model. This construction cannot be a point of departure: that would be to define the Other before hearing him speak. It would be to admit, wrongly, I think, at all levels of investigation, a rigorous codification of elements. We are still far from the mark; the general semioticity of medieval civilization (to which I have alluded) does not mean that we will not perceive, here and there, a kind of refusal to be coded.

The establishment of a model (of several partial models) will, rather, be the end of the critical process—although one cannot isolate this procedure as a particular phase of the process. By induction from the concrete traits he observes, the critic progressively elaborates the elements of this "model." He must incessantly reconsider and correct it, but it furnishes the basis in relation to which the texts define themselves and by which the coherence between them becomes manifest.

Medieval civilization in all its phases lends itself better than others to this process of modelization, precisely because it shares so many traits with what H. Berque (apropos of Islam) calls "paradigmatic" cultures. Sufficiently distant from us in time, yet not too distant; offering a relatively abundant documentation; being neither too brief nor too long; being complex but nearly devoid of irreducible contradictions, this civilization can easily be perceived, paradoxically, as a kind of historical monad: the factors that constitute it, while they are strongly redundant, transmit, when considered in their close reciprocal relationships, a considerable quantity of data. To be sure, any model tends to close upon itself; and we know that nothing in lived reality is closed. But the fiction of closure is surely, in the order of comprehension, the very condition that will permit us to think "otherness."

Thirty years ago, this process of semigeneralization was (apropos of another, not altogether separate corpus) masterfully defined by Panofsky. Everyone remembers his pages, and I can do no better than to refer the reader to them.[58]

With respect to our texts, I would suggest that no unity, internal or external, can be postulated. On this point Eugene Vance, in 1969, condemned a frequent epistemological error. Unity (if it exists) is inferred from a demonstration; but, for this very reason, it is not constituted at a very high level of generalization, but rather at that middle level where something emerges that is implied from the outset by all historical discourse by the very fact of its being a discourse: in principle that history has, or at least tends to posit, a certain order, yet this order by no means excludes the unexpected.

Thus, what I mean by "constructing a model" is "advancing a theme," carrying out a synthetic abduction with the value of a hypothesis. It is to evoke from among the observable circumstances a relationship expressed in terms that are our own, thus forcibly introducing our own historicity into the other's existence. This relationship ensures our presence on that distant horizon; it allows us to capture, with modern auditory faculties, the echoes of those lost voices. From the point of view of the now defunct positivist objectivity, such a relationship would have seemed a thing we should not admit to. But that is no longer the issue.

The "model" (I keep using this term for lack of a better one) is what makes it possible to discover the other in our pleasure. It tends to close upon itself like the portrait of a face. This is only a portrait: how could we have more than that? Our fate is that of those ancient princes who fell in love with a distant lady whose picture had been brought to them by pilgrims returning from Antioch. What we have to do is welcome travelers from Antioch and then set out, like Jaufré Rudel, without even his distant hope of dying "entre sos bratz.". . .

Thus, when I was writing my book on the Grands Rhétoriqueurs, the tapping of various sources of information led me to the gradual construction of a frame, not so much a model as a heuristic outline whose elements, without predetermining my textual choices, supplied them, overall, with a significant coherence and made it possible to infuse them, overall, with a factor of movement. Elements came alive; relations became organized; a global figure came to be reflected in the multiplicity of mirrors, trick mirrors, at times.

By purposely forcing, ever so slightly, the external givens, by exaggerating certain traits (in accord with my own sensibility, which rightfully took part in the enterprise), by putting off the moment of modulating the traits, I progressively allowed the extratextuality in which my texts were inscribed to be defined by means of six or seven parameters, manifested in several ways.

1. a progressive loss of the orality of transmission (or at the very least, the end of its absolute predominance);

2. in consequence, a reduction in the situations of potential dialogue; a reduction of the role of the voice and of bodily presence; an intervention of more and more numerous mediations, including the printed book;

3. whence a distancing of the subjects ("author"/"reader"); a discontinuity shown in innumerable social traits that attest to the distance man is taking with respect to his own body (the aversion to nudity, the invention of forks, handkerchiefs, the transformation of the diet). I was not far from deciding that this distance favored the diffusion of Aristotle's *Poetics* around 1500. . . .

4. and, on this very account, affirmation is no longer opposed to negation, but, rather, language to dissimulation;

5. geographical discoveries are pushing back the ancient frontiers around the world, places where monsters have been located; and the monsters fade from the horizon. On the other hand, blacks and Indians are discovered; the Others are no longer monstrous beings, just different men. As for the monsters, they are internalized: their place is no longer "out there," but in the depths of the very soul.

6. whence the vital need to maintain, at least fictionally, the continuity between those overthrown appearances and being it-

self: the principle motivation for the flooding of discourse by a mass of emblems. Allegory, once an effective mode of reading, has lost its original dynamism, because the level of indisputable reality to which it made reference has become fragmented and eroded, the allegorical figure no longer does anything but erroneously promote accidental qualities to the status of essence.

Within this frame, some aspects of certain texts took on more relief; others took on less. Levels formed; lines in perspective were projected toward a vanishing point: the portrait emerged as the reading went forward. In the center of the world's theatricality, the prince's Court, the theater par excellence, stood out like an elevated place, visible to all, marking the heart of the City (thanks to archaic systems of thought, artificially maintained as objects of belief or feigned belief), but not separate from it, where an action was played out, an action projected into immutable time and linked to lived reality by a relationship of analogy. On this stage, Roles incorporated all individuation into an emblematic discourse. But this discourse was double (as double as the Festival it ordained: Commemoration or Carnival); at times confirming, at times inverting things. What this discourse confirmed was the appearance of a world it held to be empty; if it inverted itself, it was in order to hold up the distorting mirror of parody, manifesting that emptiness. Or else the mirror had no backing; it was nothing but a closed window, through which the grimace of Death could be seen. Shared values, founded only on the word of the Prince, the bishop, or their spokesmen, the poets, or else on that threat of annihilation—all this inextricably mingled. A fundamental duplicity of available forms, whose bitter or ironic flavor came from that incessant circulation, from those ruptures, those movements, underneath the rhetorical rigidity and the continuity of surfaces.

§ The Temptation of the Universal

A model that lays claim to universality will be tautological or absurd. Its effectiveness can come only from its capacity to integrate and justify the unexpected, to stand against the objects it accounts for, like a deep structure against its manifestations, mediated by an open series of transformational rules. In this way two sequences of values, whose apparent contradiction is the very mark of historicity, may at the same time be opposed and united. That which, in the model, is motivated, necessary, constrained, collective, and typical appears, in the concrete text, arbitrary, aleatory, free, individual, and new. These two sequences coincide; they apply simultaneously to the same "fact"; together they constitute its verisimilitude.

That is one of the reasons there is no total history. A threat of alienation weighs upon the relationship we must make explicit between the signifier and the signified. On this point one might refer to several of Adorno's views: on the fundamental discontinuity of history, whose manifestations are necessarily fragmentary; on the very idea of "form," both as synthesis of the dispersed and negation of the total—and what is our "object," if not a form, a quantity of material, subtracted by us from the viscosity of time and solidified?[59]

For the same reason, we will never (even if one of us feels this strange need) erect a "theory of medieval texts." Over the years, all over Europe and sometimes in America, there have been enough dreams of a "theory of literature" (if not a "science of literature"!) and enough polemics on this theme that now a wise skepticism has taken hold.

What indeed is meant by the word "theory," equally polyvalent, more or less, in every domain where its usage has been introduced? At times it designates an ensemble of propositions with demonstrative status, linking into a system certain generally open classes of properties belonging to a domain of objects; at times it designates a system of hypotheses whose formulation is supposed to account for connections proper to a field of phenomena which has first been, or is in the process of being, explored and experimentally mastered; finally, at times, "theory" (and this is the strong meaning of the term) designates an ensemble of determinations characterizing the deep structure capable of unifying into a coherent system those classes of laws proper to one sector of knowledge.[60]

In none of these meanings does the word apply very well to any moment of critical reading, still less, perhaps, to the reading of texts from past eras than to that of modern texts, for the historical development of cultures (insomuch as it is apparent) rarely proceeds by linear sequences, formalizable in a closed discourse, but generally by a multidimensional expansion.

To be sure, several abstract questions, of limited number but considerable importance, call for theoretically oriented answers: the nature and functions of poetic signification; the permanence, transformations, and evanescence of poetic forms over time; cognitive structures and aesthetic emotion; the anthropological locus of poetry; and a few others.

There we have zones of elucidation, foci of critical reflection, whence this latter radiates across the reading and renders it dramatic. But we do not by any means have points of arrival. All theorization must here be understood in a very broad sense, referring to the manifestation of a learned discourse judged, by those who use it, appropriate to the heterogeneous ensemble of a certain number of realities or of specific potentialities. A poetics cannot be prevented from belonging to the order of the particular. It is related to the general only on the level of deep, individual, collective impulses, which we can scarcely conjecture when our object is a poetry of the past.

Unsatisfied with the apriority of the "operative models" in vogue, ill at ease with contradictions between rival theories, various groups of researchers up until the mid-1970s tried several times to construct a "metatheory" of the "literary fact." Such an ambition implies the idea that this "fact" is scientific in nature and is reducible to the functioning of a closed system of laws: an archaic idea, which the physicists and biologists laid aside at least thirty-five years ago. Any ensemble extracted from the real is open—which doesn't mean that it is chaotic, but the order one can discover within it is flexible, ceaselessly dissolving and reforming itself, opening onto the unimaginable.[61]

§ Concepts and Presuppositions

Marrou suggested that any discipline of a historical nature depends on five types of concepts. Two of them refer to outdated practices that are of no use to us. Three of them remain: (1) concepts pretending to universality, elaborated by generalization on the basis of a certain number of facts (to give a simple, if not simplistic, example, I might mention the triptych lyricism/drama/epic); (2) technical concepts, whose validity is limited in time and space (let's say *chanson de geste* or *laisse*); (3) concepts designating an "ideal type," whose property is that it can never be fully realized (let's say *courtoisie*).[62]

The distinction seems pertinent, at least where medieval studies are concerned. But it is no longer 1950, and today the terms defined by Marrou are the object of a psychic and ideological investment that is our own. Whence a problem which appears to be methodological, but which touches on the foundations of an epistemology. I am speaking of the very problem raised by the utilization, in reading medieval texts, of critical concepts formed and applied to the most modern texts in the course of the last thirty years, thanks to the enormous work accomplished in fields opened up by formalism, semiotics, psychoanalysis, and Marxist-inspired socio-criticism.

Inasmuch as this research allowed us to derive more or less clearly—to bring into fairly high relief—an "ideal type" of poetry, of writing, of the autoreferentiality of language, it allows us without any doubt to approach our object (whether it be a *Minnesänger* song or the *Roman de la Rose*) with more certainty than did the methods in vogue in the twenties, thirties, or even forties, methods founded on reading the *Artes dictandi*. In fact, if medieval poetry is poetry at all, it is, as such, situated at the opposite pole to what the discourse of clerics, between the eleventh and fifteenth centuries, perceived and conceptualized in language acts: truth, imitation, and ornamentation, intellective adequation—what do these have to do with the poetic phenomenon? Whence the inability of a Faral (one example among many others) to move a single step closer to that which is most intense in our old texts.

To be sure, today's critical approach to a given problematic is not in itself, in any absolute way, better than yesterday's. But it is fundamentally linked to that which is most immediate and experiential in our ways of thinking and feeling, and to that extent it is relatively better. Perhaps one or another of the propositions it offers were already posed, in apparently equivalent terms, three-quarters of a century ago. I'll grant you that it has been said before, but on the basis of another mode of knowledge. And the mode cannot be detached from the situation, or from superstructures within which any partial displacement modifies the whole—to the point where nothing but an empty form remains of that which lies immobile (on account of some refusal or some blindness) in the heart of this vast movement. I could not possibly speak about the *Chanson de Roland* as a man of the eleventh or twelfth century: why reproach me for doing so as a man of 1985 rather than 1900?

Doubtless, the "modernist" choice involves risks. We have our myths in 1985, too. . . . But that is less important than the "critical intertextuality" of which Leyla Perrone spoke a few years ago, one resulting from a genuine labor of absorption and reelaboration of other (critical) texts through and within what I write.[63]

It is regrettable that a majority of medievalists persist in ignoring this problem and in turning a blind eye to its implications. Some elude it by feigning to reduce to complexities of vocabulary any utterance that potentially questions this fundamental point. Whether there is jargon or not certainly has nothing to do with the issue, even if the absence of jargon is more pleasing; even if we must deplore, in certain circles, a sort of linguistic, if not intellectual, pollution. The only real, though surmountable, difficulty relates to the fact that "modern" critical instruments have generally been honed in the course of a reflection on contemporary, or near-contemporary, texts, which as such do not pose the problem of intercultural relations. Most of the time their study concerns history in only one of its aspects: inasmuch as it evokes the presence of the Other. Almost all the fairly heterogeneous research in question is marked in this way: engendered by Western culture of the mid-twentieth century, it is inevitably linked to the specificity of that culture, and nothing seems more dubious to me than the universality of its possible applicability.

Apparently we are at a dead end. The only way out, if there is one, lies in our practice. Can these critical instruments transcend that "cultural difference"? And if so, how? Under what methodological conditions? At the cost of what transformations? The possibility of answering these questions depends, to a large extent,

on a comparison, philological in nature, between the circumstances surrounding the production of objects: the modern object
and the medieval object. These circumstances are of every sort,
and their description requires a certain interdisciplinarity: some are
socioeconomic; others are technological, ideological, phantasmal,
aesthetic. . . . On all these levels resemblances and differences appear, but each one of them may be either apparent or functional
(the forms of modern gestures of politeness stem in part from old
chivalric rites, but their function is altogether different). The same
holds on the textual level. Whence a double necessity at every
moment of reading the medieval text: to discover the formal
marks whereby the text inserted itself into the culture of its time;
simultaneously, to redefine, adapt, and at times to reject modern
critical concepts in such a way as to enable them to grasp this
historicity.

I will allege, as an example, the notion of *text*, indispensable
today, as much from the linguistic point of view as in relation to
poetics or the critique of ideologies. In the material sense, the
objects of our gaze are medieval texts. But several factors converge
to render their definition different from that of a modern text:

the complexity of the very act of writing (difficulty of handling
the tools, expensiveness);

specificity of the possible motivations for the act (patronage,
commemoration, propaganda) and for the censorships that oppose
it;

low frequency of the act; relative rarity of the book, object of
artisanal fabrication doubtless devoid of economic benefit;

poor diffusion (printing would not noticeably alter this state of
things until the sixteenth century);

inability to read, in most of the public, either from lack of
books or from illiteracy;

auditory consumption of the majority of texts: through an inter-
posed public reading, through recitation by memory, or through
oral improvisation.

We could easily prolong this list, to which we must add all the
factors of the text's *mouvance*—even if it affects only a part of
medieval poetry. At least, the traits indicated here reveal, among
other things, that the medieval text is much closer than the

modern text to the body of the person who performs it (author, reciter, singer) and the person who receives it (listener or reader). The medieval text, much more than the modern one, is gesture, action, charged with sensory elements. Its relation to the sender and to the receiver is necessarily other, and more concrete.

Another example: "writing" (*écriture*), a term which, in the last fifteen years' criticism, especially in France, has often been used to refer to a kind of autonomous entity, has lost its first denotation as a scriptural act. Everything that has been said about what constitutes writing in particular practice, about the dispersion it effects on the terms of communicative action, all this represents a conceptual gain that we can ignore only at our peril. However, the word "writing" also designates an ensemble of historically conditioned phenomena, which have a determining, though variable, influence on the intensity of its effects:

writing is the manual operation that consists of tracing characters, by means of some instrument, on a material furnished for that purpose; this operation supposes an intention of deferred communication, beyond a determined space and time;

writing is also the complex of conditions and circumstances of this operation (biological, psychological, sociological, etc.);

finally, writing designates globally the result of the operation thus conditioned and situated.

Each of these elements demands to be redefined at each moment of history. The French *chansons de geste*, put in writing in the twelfth, thirteenth, and fourteenth centuries, must certainly have had a previous, perhaps even a subsequent, period of oral transmission; several analogies borrowed from other "paradigmatic" cultures would lead us to believe that at least some of these songs were initially produced orally ("improvisationally"?). Thus, one may not speak, in regard to them, about an original "putting in writing." Nonetheless (as I think I showed in 1963 in *Langue et techniques poétiques*), the effect of "deferred communication" was produced, in the performance itself, by the use of a quasi-ritualistic language. Orality, to be sure, linked the spoken text to a *hic et nunc*, inserted it within a presence: but this presence found itself torn from its concrete temporal and spatial conditions, because it promoted a mythic image of the society in which the singer and his listeners all participated. By the time our manuscripts were produced, one or two centuries later, the operation of setting them down in writing acted to provoke a second effect of distancing and of communicative dispersion: this second effect, founded on the first one, sharpened it, corrected it, or replaced it by superimposing itself upon it.

Still another example: the notion of "intertextuality" is one that is potentially productive for the medievalist, if he gives it nuance (for it functions on several levels) and distinguishes it very clearly, on the one hand, from the biologizing idea of "sources" and, on the other, more subtly, from the medieval concept of *imitatio*. Indeed, these terms are not interchangeable. "Intertextuality" seems much more useful in accounting for what we think today about the texts' mode of existence. As for the word *imitatio*, it designates, in the medieval period, the reproduction within a text, occasionally by means proper to figurative artists, of a rationalized *ordo*. That is, *imitatio* operates through reason. It is the conformity of a certain poetic or pictorial discourse to an order conceived by reason, a conformity that respects *convenientia*, that is, a certain verisimilitude within the text.

It would be interesting, and not impossible, similarly to establish a corrective lexicon of the terms most frequent in modern textual analysis. But such a lexicon would have only a relative value, for our Middle Ages represent a long slice of history, and (even taking into account the stability of many of its structures) the circumstances of a twelfth-century text are not identical to those of a fifteenth-century one: "medieval culture," though more homogeneous than ours, was not monolithic. A redefinition must take place on the level of each text or class of texts.

This does not mean, of course, naively skimming off a layer of fashionable vocabulary or bowing humbly to all the university's advertising slogans. . . . A critical discourse is valid only insomuch as, being constructed, it is deconstructed, in order to be reconstructed through self-criticism. It must take into account the "discovery" and the myths that give it coherence. Our only chance to overcome, in our speech, the ascendancy of a language originating elsewhere than in us lies in opening ourselves up to it, again and again, being ourselves subjects both determined (thus, not original) and determining (thus, necessary).

The fact that all discourse implies presuppositions is in itself a matter of indifference. What counts is discovery, imposition of meaning, and articulation in time (if we agree on emblematically reducing the medievalist's model-task to this scheme): there are that many levels of presupposition. Concepts put in play by any work of thought that transforms a fragment of the universe into a theme are certainly not in themselves, or in the same operation, subject to this transformation. Still, it is important to make the concepts explicit. And nowadays this desirable explicitness is more rarely found among medievalists than among other historians or critics, to the point that people have playfully wondered whether their specialty may not be founded on a fear of the maxim "Know thyself."

§ In Search of a Face

The ultimate validity, the practical effectiveness of a notion, and, even more, of a theoretical proposition, is related to the strength of the roots it sinks into reality and to the flow of inductive sap that keeps feeding them. Every attempt at generalization or expli-cation, every search for causes, every effort to unveil deep func-tions and the procedures they put in motion take on meaning only in and through the work of information gathering, which accom-panies and nourishes those functions and which, in turn, is made fertile by them.

Several people of my generation or the next forgot at times this banal truth, in favor of a metaphysics that failed to declare its name. Doubtless we are thereby collectively responsible, willy-nilly, for the "fed up" state we observe in many of our students, for their disinterest in the weight, color, and flavor of things; for their distrust of the apparent security that comes from a sensation of ground beneath one's feet, even if it is made of sand or mud; for their lack of appetite for texts, because texts are the issue. . . .

Victims, it is said, of the mass media: perhaps because, in our eyes, the latter are emblematic of the decline of that memorialized capital that distinguished persons used to call, and still called a few years ago, "culture." This capital was deposited in a select number of books, in the brains of recognized masters, in a few organized disciplines (that is, in the very thing fixed by the Middle Ages through the practice of the "liberal arts"!). Its income was paid to us in the form of elaborate discourses with virtually eternal validity. What difference does any of this make to our youth? A sure instinct reveals to them the elements that link this learning to the most entrenched prejudices of a society they want nothing to do with. Why should we be surprised by their rejection?

It is up to us, while there is still time, to reinvent, on other grounds, in another perspective, and with another ethic, different discourses, both constructed and common, capable of exposing our true problems and thus enabling us to go beyond the conflicts that paralyze us. If we do not restore to their former preeminent place the slow, ungrateful labor of data gathering, the collection of documents, the sometimes irksome initial reading (combing the text), then we must consent to renouncing everything, because there will no longer be anything to say in the midst of these buried treasures that mutely call out to us. Flattened, crushed onto the paper or parchment by the heavy weight of centuries, what they expect from us is that we give them back their volume: but how can we undertake that with any chance of success, before having attentively picked up the trail and measured the remains, inventoried the site, dated the strata?

True, among all specialists in texts, it is medievalists who have been least affected by the general disaffection from learning; but if they were preserved from it, it was more through inertia than through will. Besides, not everyone was preserved from it: in some sectors of our studies and in some countries and some schools more than in others, there can still occasionally be found a sort of uncertainty with respect to the once dominant erudite learning; people are yielding, tardily, to the prestige of other virtues, borrowed from linguistics or from semiology, which makes for a philology ashamed of its age; wrongly ashamed, for as Pierre Guiraud used to remind us, a learning that has held up for centuries can perfectly well be judged false in theory while remaining usable in practice, if certain precautions are taken. This would lead us back to the inverse danger, which we will avoid on pain of leaving unchanged the essence of the deep intentions.

It is not a question of denying the considerable gains of a century's erudition, whatever its distortions may have been, nor of closing down this always open building site, but still less is it a question of the opposite excess: taking already assured knowledge and annexing it, without nuance, to a contemporary ideology. There are other things to read, and to read otherwise. Bereft of theoretical reinforcements, erudition gets lost in the sands of memory. It nonetheless has its own function (for which nothing can be substituted), which is to uncover one by one the elements of the "cultural milieu" and, to a lesser extent, of the "textual space." The historian of "medieval literature" does not labor in vain when he succeeds in proving that around 1060, in Spain, a version of the *Chanson de Roland* was known. The discovery is not in question; what is in question is the fate of the knowledge it engenders, the awareness we must have that factual data fulfills a necessary condition of every critical reading: the respective place-ment of the object and its observer.

To be sure, the facts uncovered by erudition are never anything but "facts" produced, as I have reminded the reader, by our discourses, valid as long as the propositional relationships constitut-ing those discourses remain stable; this is all the more true in the case of experiences in which we no longer participate. The decep-tive innocence of our forebears led them to more than one description, more than one definition, inadmissible today, which forged a creature of reason or of thin air, whose methodological usefulness we can no longer allow. Witness, among many hasty constructions of a supposedly biographical nature, the perfectly circular tautologies to which a reading of a text still leads, for some old-fashioned individuals (as a notable and symptomatic example, most studies devoted to Villon's *Testament*). Witness those recon-structions of an "authentic version" that used to be produced; witness the methods of dating founded on "allusions" made by the author to "historical facts," often problematic ones (I am thinking of the romancer Gautier d'Arras, even of Chrétien de Troyes, objects of chronologizing polemics that ought to be critically analyzed!).

Close attention must be paid at every moment to indispensable revisions; the "fact" for us is exactly what specifies this attention, not as a reasoned object, as has been said, but as a "limit of the thinkable."[64] At least the foundations remain, which we would be wrong to mistake for rubbish to be discarded: techniques of the most practical kind; an ancient and glorious philology, a whole set of tools for validating the reality of texts, for attesting it, for making it credible.

It is through erudition that the discovery of otherness must pass. And from otherness comes the pleasure; there is pleasure only in the Other, a concrete, historical Other. Pleasure carries a trace of history: if my object is a loved woman, history is there in the very fact that she exists, *hic et nunc*. If the object is a medieval text, I must come to know its body; but that body will be uncovered for me only after my information is as complete as it can be.

Whence, once more, the only true problem: how to articulate the first knowledge I have of this being, with a comprehension implying the demystifying recognition, on my part, of my own historicity? Not in the idealist sense of the *subtilitas applicandi* of hermeneutist theologians, but in the sense of accounting for the implications of my research (on the axis *ego-hic-nunc*) as I conduct it; an integration, in accord with my own conscience, of the fact that my historical knowledge is irreducibly mediated. Why, on the strength of what socio-historical motivations, did men communicate with other men thanks to, and by means of, a given form? Who communicated with whom? Wasn't the cultural milieu visible in the texts camouflaged, on various pretexts, by the scribes who constituted them, in association with a narrow ruling class? It is up to us to find within them the traces of a conflict between several coexisting forces: the factors alternately predominant and the quest for a meeting in the heart of the contradiction. Here ideologies situate themselves, rival systems of representation, reflecting a society's antagonisms in the same way as other simultaneous and no less distorting systems; no less protective, finally— and incessantly deformed by a nearly irreducible distance between referential systems and effective behaviors: a gap to which nothing at that time could give a name.[65]

On this level, as well as the other, the area for necessary labor remains wide open. Too many documents are still to be inventoried, published, reread, resituated. A labor in the field, within the enormous mass of raw materials, requiring adequate utilization of the critical instruments elaborated by the human sciences, but, also, the will to historicize these materials by replacing them in the complex fabric of their time. A labor in two phases. First phase: to unite the manifestations of a single phenomenon, both as it was once produced and lived, and as it is conceptualized by the researcher. Second phase: to regroup that series into a greater unity, rational in nature.

Thus, I do not mean to designate as "erudition" the mere harvesting of documents linked traditionally to an ostentatious humility with regard to its material. Exhaustiveness of information is, in fact, not only impossible; it is inconceivable. The data are by nature fragmentary; the erudition that proceeds to a first classification of the givens has incompleteness as its very essence. Thus, it will consist, for the medievalist, not so much in patching gaps and filling up holes as in articulating each fragment within the series to which it belongs, either by projecting quantitative elements or by extrapolating a signifying effect. The passage from documentation to interpretation, from documentary writing to the reading that will thereby be given to history, thus moves from a term that is *in reality* fragmentary to an end that is *potentially* totalizing.

On this very point the remains of a classical conception of unity within the oeuvre lastingly beclouded medieval studies. A series of metaphors (whose status as such was lost sight of) a priori posed the "oeuvre" as a living organism. Whence the need to describe it as a closed and autonomous whole and, when the text eluded the grasp, interventions practiced in the name of a debased philology: medievalists treated in the light (if I can call it that!) of a critical experience worthy of the late nineteenth century innumerable texts that were composite, filled with gaps, or (at times, supposedly) unfinished or hypertrophic: the *Chanson de Guillaume*, the *Conte du Graal* . . . or the *Jeu d'Adam*, from which, for purposes of simplication, the long poem ending the manuscript was cut. Ambiguities that should have been left as such were made into causalities and were played off against one another in order to restore the "truth," of which there is only one, by definition. For even among those people influenced, around 1950, by the formalist temptation, this complex of prejudices was readopted in the perspective of a structuralist totalization.

Our task, instead, (who can seriously doubt it today?) is to grasp the places of rupture, the points of breakdown: our own fragmentation, brought about by reading. . . .

§ Pluralism

This exigency itself creates the need for that pluralism of information invoked at the beginning of this book. In a sense close to this one, Jacques Le Goff speaks of "reasoned eclecticism and successive skiddings." After a century and a half of research, there is a question we can no longer ignore. Namely, once the procedures thus constituted have brought about the necessary analytic decomposition, must this in turn bring about the decomposition of our object in a general atomization? Once the diverse characteristics of the object have been set apart (an indispensable move at the outset), must this setting apart finally exact the highest cost of all: impossibility of interdisciplinary communication, and dislocation of knowledge into "a thousand ignorant bits of learning," as Edgar Morin puts it? These are the very limitations that contemporary thought in general refuses to accept.[66] Perhaps the collective mentality of our contemporaries (all of them, and we medievalists with them) is returning, after traversing every imaginable transformation, to a mental attitude comparable to that of the Middle Ages: a profound conviction that every thing, every life, every history, makes, or at least tries to make, sense. Whence an irrepressible need for interpretation, strong enough to channel the most heterogeneous pieces of data and reactualize them on the level of our present preoccupations: a universal tendency, it seems to me, today in so-called technological civilization. A "primitive" tendency, which a scholar ought not to oppose but to tame and submit to rational control without repressing it.

Deep structures that emerge within a circumscribed event become delimited by approximation, in successive and theoretically distinct approaches. Without risking an illusory globalization, let's not cease to shift the elements of the scenery; let's refuse to allow closure, to the point where ideological frameworks begin, at least, to fall apart, and the screen by which they isolate us begins to dissipate.

What we construct in this way is a scaffolding of hypotheses tending toward the interpretation of an *idea* of a text, in the fifteenth-century meaning of that word: relative to the form of the body, to perceptible appearance, to fundamental traits of the species. Hypotheses organized in a double series, depending on whether they converge into, or escape from, a synthesizing view: so that these multiple discourses on the same "fact" actualize it in different, perhaps even contradictory, events. Dislocating different problematics, constraining various methods to overlap one another, the critical reader of medieval texts knows he will never be able to procure a seat from which he can take in the whole drama, its functioning, its machinery, and the words spoken by the masked players.

It is not so much a matter of starting from prefabricated methods as of rejecting any simplification, and rejecting disjunctions when they turn out empirically to be misleading. Erudition today can only be inter- (or rather trans-) disciplinary. In fact, it breaks the pure linearity of causes and effects, and tends to pose the event (text) as a signifying entity, ungraspable in itself, of course, but whose every manifestation constitutes a signal. We will not succeed in circumscribing this entity, for it is perhaps itself no more than a creature of reason (but of *our* reason). At least we will summon to the task the greatest possible number of those correlative and unstratifiable disciplines designated by the perhaps contradictory expression "human sciences."

It is impossible to deny that, at the basis of the dreams which animate this intellectual attitude, there is a distant utopian memory (*de omni re scibili*). Let us be aware of it, and be cautious. Moreover, it should be understood that I am pleading neither for amateurism, with its perpetual mystifications, nor for some juxtaposition of mutual ignorances.[67] I am advocating instead a radicalization of specialized disciplines, self-renewed, critical of their content, ascetically riveted to their concrete object, while denying any totalizing pretension. It is also true that somewhere pluralism comes up against boundaries: the very ones that limit the universality, the unity, and the pertinence of significations. It is historical conditions that impose those boundaries. The admirable ambiguity of many medieval texts, and the generous diffusion of meaning that emanates from them, should not permit us completely to dilute our reading of them. They require instead the enunciation of a discourse in tension against the institutional constraints that force it to repeat and incessantly reproduce itself, for it refuses to be made into a purely exteriorized fact.

One could maintain that inter- or trans-disciplinary pluralism functions most of all on the level of the "concepts with claims to universality" of which Marrou spoke. By accumulating fundamental observations, it lets them be invalidated, or confirmed and refined, and thus made more credible; whence their critical effectiveness.

The text remains nonetheless in *mouvance*: a fragment of itself, and never the same, a fundamental mutability scarcely hidden by a mask of organicity, in somewhat the same way as "I" constitute the unitary and fictional mask of that series of fragments that was my existence. We have, then, a plurality of significant unknowns of which it is doubtful that all may be identified, either synchronically or diachronically. Whence the precautions that must be taken in the perilous passages of such an itinerary:

1. at the moment of testing the competencies brought to bear in the various prospected fields; ambivalent competencies, indispensable to the validity of general conclusions, but always threatening, by their inherent weight, to slow my progress toward generalization;

2. at the moment of crossing the boundaries of a specialized discipline into the transdisciplinary: a crossing which implies break-

ing a routine (hence, an element of security), and which operates on a level of conceptualization that is difficult to determine a priori;

3. in the course of the transfer of terminologies, a transfer that cannot help engendering—if only through its metaphorical uses—ambitions to dominate on one side or another of the demarcation line.

In any case, in the universe we live in, we no longer have ownership rights over any critical discourse, whatever its constituent factors, because it acts from now on against what is ownable. That is why the question that was fashionable not long ago, "Where are you coming (speaking) from?" does not ring true in this instance. It supposes a topographical certainty that I do not possess; it makes me both a partner and an arbiter of a stabilizable situation. The answer can only be declarative: I am coming neither from here nor from there; the ground on this work site is shifting under my feet.

§§§§§§·

The Narrator of History

Each of the two historicities that meet in a critical reading of the medieval work are invested in a text: target-text and gloss-text function together as the thing interpreted and as the interpretant. The relationship between the one and the other is established in two moments: the writing-reading and the reading-writing. Whatever I write, be it an article of several pages or notes for a talk, there will be this double passage: from the writing of the document, now my object, a language act inscribed in a material system and in several constituent time spans (the time it took to write, the writer's personal time, the centuries between him and me, and finally our modernity) to the reading I attempt with my writing, proposing to decipher this document as text and as history.

The reading is situated both in what was the horizon of expectation for Others, forever lost, and for me; in the writing, on one end of that chain, speaks a discourse whose intentionality I don't know and whose determinants I can only partially grasp; at the other end speaks my own writing, laden with who I am, in conformity with the language I have inherited. Writing-reading, reading-writing: a play of mirrors catching the reflection of dead values in the glass of lived values, *per speculum in aenigmate*. . . . The lines that I trace are not finally reduced to their intentional function of gloss: they constitute the place of exchange between two force fields, that of the text read and that of my text that reads, which will in turn be read. I pronounce a new discourse, still in a state of becoming, heavy with implications, many of which I barely know, and add it to a discourse suspended in its state of irremediable incompleteness.

Thus, my text attempts to narrate the Other, emblazoned *en abîme* on this "field." My text is written, doubly so. Marrou pointed out that all historical knowledge naturally entails a narrative formulation, precisely on account of its social function. Moreover, it is becoming evident today that all theorization, even a partial one, tends to institute the equivalent of a myth, and that critical discourse, whatever its degree of abstraction, does not fail to convey particles of narrative.

"Narrative," in this context, refers to a rationality of discourse, an ordering of what has been retained as "facts." It refers to an intelligibility, certainly more limited, as we are reminded once again by Marrou, than that claimed by the author of a novel or a "historical" drama,[68] but fundamentally of the same kind. It is a narrative devoid, at least in intention, of naiveté; an interrogatory narrative, reintroducing in the second or in the third degree the polysemy of its object.

It is true that among practitioners of pure historical research we see a desire to be free of narrative. What inspires the desire is none other than a critical reaction against that tradition (of Greco-Roman origin, confirmed in the Middle Ages) which made of historiography a narrative of narratives, reproducing itself indefinitely in quest of some moral significance. The elimination of all narrative elements constitutes nonetheless little more than a phantasmal goal.

Our discourse contains three levels of reality, each one as fleeting and uncertain as the others: that of the events (for us, the medieval texts), that of history as such, and that of the text that *we* are writing. The first creates the third, which interprets the second, which makes the first perceptible. The "moment" of interpretation necessarily implies, with respect to the raw series of delimited events, a reduction manifested textually in the guise of a narrative scheme, more or less subtle and avowed.[69]

This secondary structuration of the referential, this specific *mimesis* stemming in part from what Lucette Finas calls "excess" in reading, is fictional in nature. The secret desire for totalization, to which I have already alluded, deeply inscribed in historical reading

88

(although nowadays repressed) emerges less through the grandiose rhetorical ambitions harbored not long ago by a Toynbee or a Curtius than—more indirectly—through the fiction inherent in any narrative speech.

However, the narrative order (the fiction constituted by my reading of the text) is not identified as such with the narrative order engendered by the writing. Whence a break in what I write: all the more marked because, for the reasons I have here recalled, we have had to reject, even denounce, our former mentors' obsession with everything that polishes, unifies, patches over, lubricates; we have had to denounce their calm horror of everything that slips, escapes, perversely multiplies, disguises itself, tells lies: that is, of life itself. On the contrary, our task is to take up that dialogic critical discourse of which Roland Barthes spoke, one that grasps the points of rupture and identifies the places where the real breaks forth. A discontinuous narrative with broken semantic lines, a mixture of science and fiction, in which the latter alone makes the former rich and communicable: my narrative transforms the "fact," which it resolves into a *thing done*; in the read text it uncovers an action.

Such is my fiction, whose referentiality stems not so much from a claim to authenticity as from the subordination of the narrative syntax to a constructed model, whose function is to make the syntax intelligible as such. Initially, the fact serves as a clue; and the purpose of the discourse is the coherent organization of a certain number of signifiers. The object of my critical language, as both an "effect of the real" and a thing-not-said, is maintained in an unstable position. What more can I do without slipping into metaphysics? Whatever I write about this old text that I love is only a provisional transition between me and it, that Other definitively absent from our community, except in my discourse. The com-prehension to which I aspire stems from a desire that is capable of suspending the effect of otherness; but my discourse, for all its documentary resources and its rhetoric, will succeed only in enunciating the other's verisimilitude, to make a place for him in you and me. Making explicit my own rapport with the past, this discourse set the scene for the other in our present: it does not recreate what is dead.

§ Dialogism and Allegory

A dialogic critical discourse. . . . A narrative never concluded. Is it not in these terms that writers of the Middle Ages spoke of ancient texts (in the same position for them as the medieval texts for us)? Copying, rewriting, glossing, moralizing by means of the multiple analogies through which that world represented itself, in a commentary that was incessant, open, perpetually reopened onto an actual and changing audience, simultaneously playing several games on several levels. What idealist hermeneutics as well as early structuralism neglected in what *we* read was precisely those nonsensical senses, those specular images, those inconsistent terms that medievalists easily dispensed with by blaming them on errors of transmission.

Will conservatives accuse us of creating confusion? Let us rather invoke the obliqueness of discourse, the rejection of that mono-semy in which traditional "scientific" medievalism tried to enclose itself, without ever having proven (no more than other disciplines of the time) the least connection between singleness of meaning and validity of knowledge. We reject this repressive scientism.[70]

If, just as I reject a facile agnosticism, I also emphasize the fictional aspect of the text we write, it is because there is no truth: or because there is not one truth, which amounts to the same thing.

In principle we know that. But a long mental habit still leads us, the minute we relax our critical control, to suppose a binary character, true or false, in the content of any discourse. On the level of raw information, of actual archeology, historiography certainly involves truth or error, and the former is preferable. But aside from the fact that it is often difficult to draw a boundary between them (because erudition, luckily, never ceases to contest it), the transition to narrative, implying interpretation, forces us out of those categories. The "fact," both given as known and implied in the discursive operation, is no longer anything but one constituent element of a dynamic signification, charged with ten-sions that could be concealed only by means of a fallacious rhetoric. The truth *asserts* its authority only to the detriment of mean-ing.[71]

Let us acknowledge that between the "facts" there is a diversity of relationships, both vertical and horizontal: resemblances, dif-ferences, proportions, conjunctions, disjunctions, interferences. . . . But let us resist thinking about them in terms of *causality*; let us prefer a relationship of *analogy*, which leaves more margin, so to speak, for the freedom in history: *non verum sed verisimile*, Abelard taught around 1130; analogy, less an explanatory procedure than a heuristic mode. What discourse can we use, then, except the one in whose spaces that otherwise irretrievable reality lies in wait, the discourse which stretches out toward that limit, that other status of meaning, while knowing it can never be attained?

Thus, from the socio-historical context to the poetic idea man-ifested in the text, and to the structures of the text (including its phono-syntactic organization), historicity is precisely that shifting network of analogies that unify these elements, in the same way as, for a thirteenth-century contemplative, other analogies linked the microcosm to the macrocosm, the human soul to the starry sky, assuring their coherence in an incessant cosignification.

How, if we needed to, would we characterize this discourse, this scarcely definable thing, this narrative bearing its own gloss, this abstract figuration that relates to a constructed model those ele-ments of the text as perceived in its unity? I would not hesitate to speak of an *allegorical* discourse, if the word had not become devalued (wrongly so): "allegorical" precisely inasmuch as any gen-eralizing vision overlies (but does not penetrate) the concrete, polymorphic, polysemic text, heavy with latent affectivity and sexuality. This vision takes in the text in its abstract projections (the only ones conceivable) in order to reconstruct it as a utopian narrative. In the end, it is allegory that seems to account for our ambiguous relationship to history, for what is the secondary rela-tionship of narrative to concept, fiction to science. It would be futile to protest. Here too we are following (though wearing other shoes, and on another level) the path of our old medieval pre-decessors. It seems to me that this explains why the medievalist critic (quite apart from the character of his writing or the profundity of his thought) appears irreducibly marginal to the society in which he lives: it explains his fundamental exteriority and, in a tangential way, his freedom in the face of "undiscoverable history," as it has been called. Torn between my present and this past to which my existence has committed me, I travel across the long experience of a practice that is both my own and someone else's. Whence the uncertainty; whence the fables through which I try to exhaust a necessity. All I aspire to is that finally, after me, the uncertainty be resolved, absorbed by the necessity.

§ Gai Savoir

As Roland Barthes said in his inaugural lecture, "it is the taste for words that makes learning fruitful." Following Marc Bloch, we would oppose to a "cold" learning a "warm" learning, one that brings hope. Beyond the self-interested half-truths peddled by the nineteenth century and by a good portion of our own, we find ourselves confronting an apparently obvious fact: the profound unity of critical discourse and poetry. Manifestations of the one and the other emanate from the same thrust of desire, the same appetite; they end at the same cutoff point, the same retreat, the same *co-naissance*, in Claudel's pun, the one and the other founders of the only myths we really need in order to live.[72]

Both criticism and poetry are animated by the same tension between an order, wrongly confused with what is real, and an apparent disorder in what is lived. This tension results from a "contextual simultaneity," and because of its transgressive dynamism, with every written sentence, causes (should, could cause . . .) the breakdown of all tolerance for ideological discourse and reigning clichés.[73] And both criticism and poetry "exploit" the text they trace, "oppress" it, and draw blood and water from it in order that their violence may triumph.

Indeed, it is not without violence (against the inertia of our traditions, against the weight of circumstances, against myself) that I overhear echoes of those few past words. They still resound (or was I mistaken?) like the ocean in a shell, within the hollow of the texts which I am, as they say "looking into": yes, looking into that being I already love without knowing it, into that body within which, through which, once it is "laid bare," the universe will reveal itself, presence and obstacle against which I will be broken.

The only thing that justifies the effort of our reading is the pleasure it gives us. Philippe Verdier used to tell me that Focillon, in his courses at the Collège de France, spoke about *happiness*. I prefer *pleasure*, maybe because of Barthes, and because of the connotations that enrich the word. The pleasure of being confronted with historical knowledge, in an apparent mutual refusal—a tension and, once again, a rupture between two different ends which, however, could never be separated without ruining the whole enterprise. Doubtless one of them (pleasure) is located at a greater distance than the other (knowledge), but isn't that enough to make us condemn those among us whose learning is "sad" and exalt the *gay saber* exemplified for us by the last troubadours? For in the end what is learning if not a poetic object (though it does not thus cease to be learning), poetic in the strongest sense that may be given to the word?

Knowledge (that is, our "human sciences") functions for us at the source of that pleasure, in the same way as an archetypic story functions for people of other societies—as "sacred history" for people of the Middle Ages. However, it would be fallacious to mark stages, a progression, a chronology between those terms of equivocality: the irreplaceable and delicious equivocality of the inexhaustible.

Whatever we do, we will never possess anything. That much we know. What remains is the derisive freedom to trace signs on paper, a small thing, like the designs in the naked twigs on a maple tree under my window. They are pretending to have caught the whole winter sky in their net—and who knows? Perhaps they really have caught it.

Notes

1. Translator's note: *Les sciences humaines* does not correspond to any division of disciplines current in the United States. It refers to a combination of social sciences and humanities, particularly those fields—philosophy, linguistics, ethnology, social history—studied at the Ecole Pratique des Hautes Etudes in Paris.

2. See the review of papers and discussions at the Centre Georges-Pompidou in *Perspectives médiévales* 5 (1979); see Planche, 1976, and Combarieu, 1979; on an epistemological level, Jauss, 1977a, 9–47.

3. Le Goff, 1977, 10–11; Le Goff, 1978.

4. Graus, 1975; Friedländer, 1975, 145.

5. Friedell, 1946, I, 13; cf. Gadamer, 1976, 147. On the medieval idea of the past, see Gässmann, 1974.

6. Zumthor, 1983, esp. 79–146.

7. Legendre, 1974, esp. 50–115.

8. See particularly the recent work of Dragonetti, 1980, 1982; and Méla, 1984, 11–22.

9. Certeau, 1975, 43–44.

10. Warning, 1975, 7.

11. Gumbrecht, 1977.

12. Badel, 1974, 246.

13. Zumthor, in *Mittelalterliche Studien*, 1984, 301–12.

14. Fichant, 1969, 102–3.

15. Charles, 1977, 25.

16. Marrou, 1954, 26–28.

17. Jauss, 1977a, 359–66; Le Goff, 1977, 19–45.

18. Todorov, 1978a, 13–16; Lacoue-Labarthe and Nancy, 1978, 27; on all these questions, see Mouralis, 1975.

19. Jauss, 1979; Friedländer, 1975, 12–14 and 159; cf. Whyte, 1962.

20. Corti, 1978; Haidu, 1977.

21. Cf. Stempel and Kosellek, 1973.

22. White, 1973.

23. Patte, 1978, 18–20.

24. Ouspenski, 1976.

25. Todorov, 1978a, 47–82.

26. Badel, 1974, 259–63.

27. Todorov, 1978a, 45; Lacoue-Labarthe and Nancy, 1978, 26; Charles, 1977, 10–15.

28. *Mittelalterliche Studien*, 1984, 9–13.

29. Cf. Milner, 1978, 44–45.

30. Zumthor, 1978.

31. Reiss, 1979.

32. Jauss, 1979; cf. Brunner, Conze, and Kosellek, 1972.

33. Jauss, 1970; Köhler, 1977.

34. Jimenez, 1973, 318.

35. *Mittelalterliche Studien*, 1984, 301–12.

36. Moser, 1979; Todorov, 1978a, 17–18.

37. Jauss, 1979.

38. Stierle, 1977; Milner, 1978, 51; Todorov, 1978b, 91–156; cf. Dakyns, 1973.

39. *Diskurs der Literatur*, 1983, 49–71, 280–301, 333–65.

40. Furet, 1974, 59–60; Krauss, 1959; Jauss, 1978, 21–80.

41. Jauss, 1977b, 324.

42. Greimas, 1976, 29.

43. Goux, 1978, 175.

44. Kirckpatrick, 1978.

45. Jauss, 1977b, 329–30.

46. Jauss, 1979; Serres, 1968, 21–35; Lohner, 1978.

47. Limentani, 1978.

48. Prieto, 1971; Eco, 1971; Vance, 1979; Barthes, 1978, 22.

49. By *mouvance* I mean to indicate that any work, in its manuscript tradition, appears as a constellation of elements, each of which may be the object of variations in the course of time or across space. The notion of *mouvance* implies that the work has no authentic text properly speaking, but that it is constituted by an abstract scheme, materialized in an unstable way from manuscript to manuscript, from performance to performance.

50. A team led by J. Le Goff and J. Cl. Schmitt at the Ecole Pratique des Hautes Etudes de Sciences Sociales is currently working on medieval gestural systems.

51. Zumthor, 1975, 163–215; Jauss, 1977b, 328.

52. Leclercq, Talbot, and Rochais, 1957, I, I, 11. This is a free translation.

53. Cf. Gagnon, 1977, 32–37.

54. Instead, I refer the reader to vol. 36 of *Poétique*, in which all the articles present considerations directly applicable to this context. See also Rossman, 1975.

55. Baroja, 1965.

56. Cf. Charles, 1977, 60; Patte, 1978, 16–17; Valesio, 1978, 1–8.

57. Meschonnic, 1978, 403.

58. Panofsky, 1957, chap. 1.

59. Veyne, 1971, 111 and 203–5; Le Roi Ladurie, 1973, 171; Jimenez, 1973, 200–204.

60. Ruprecht, 1978, 8; Valesio, 1978.

61. Greimas and Courtes, 1979, article on "Theory."

62. Marrou, 1954, 143–59.

63. Perrone-Moisés, 1976.

64. Certeau, 1975, 99; cf. Méla, 1978, 113–27.

65. Gourevitch, 1983, and, in a

more specific way, Le Goff, 1981, illustrate types of research on these points.

66. Cf. Le Goff, 1977, 109–10; Morin, 1977, 33–67.

67. Cf. Meschonnic, 1978, 417.

68. Marrou, 1954, 30, 44–45.

69. See the contributions of H. Weinrich and K. Stierle in Stempel and Koselleck, 1973, 519–29 and 530–34; cf. Friedländer, 1975, 38–40.

70. Serres, 1982, 150–194.

71. Cf. Serres, 1968, 24.

72. Cf. Marin, 1973, 18–35, 44–50.

73. Stierle, 1977, 430–31.

—

Works Cited

Badel, P. Y. 1974. "Pourquoi une poétique médiévale?" *Poétique* 18:246–64.

Baroja, J. C. 1965. *El Carnaval: Analisi socio-cultural.* Madrid: Taurus.

Barthes, R. 1978. *Leçon.* Paris: Seuil.

Brunner, O., W. Conze, and R. Koselleck. 1972. *Geschichtliche Grundbegriffe.* Stuttgart: E. Klett.

Certeau, M. de. 1975. *L'Ecriture de l'histoire.* Paris: Gallimard.

Charles, M. 1977. *Rhétorique de la lecture.* Paris: Seuil.

Combarieu, M. de. 1979. "Le Moyen Âge et Radio-France." *Perspectives médiévales* 5:16–27.

Corti, M. 1978. "Structures idéologiques et structures sémiotiques au XIIIe siècle." *Travaux de linguistique et de littérature* 16:93–105.

Dakyns, J. R. 1973. *The Middle Ages in French Literature, 1850–1900.* London: Oxford University Press.

Diskurs der Litteratur—und Sprachhistorie. 1983. Edited by B. Cerquiglini and H. V. Gumbrecht. Frankfurt: Suhrkamp.

Dragonetti, R. 1980. *La Vie de la lettre au moyen âge.* Paris: Seuil.

———. 1982. *Le Gai Savoir dans la rhétorique courtoise.* Paris: Seuil.

Eco. U. 1971. *Le Forme del contenuto.* Milan: Bompiani.

Fichant, M. 1969. "L'idée d'une histoire des sciences." *Sur l'histoire des sciences.* Edited by M. Fichant and M. Picheux. Paris: P.U.F.

Friedell, E. 1946. *Kulturgeschichte der Neuzeit.* Munich: C. H. Beck.

Friedländer, S. 1975. *Histoire et psychanalyse.* Paris: Seuil.

Furet, F. 1974. "Le Quantitatif en histoire." *Faire de l'histoire.* Vol. I. Edited by J. Le Goff and P. Nora. Paris: Gallimard. Pp. 42–61.

Gadamer, H. G. 1976. *Vérité et méthode.* Paris: Seuil.

Gagnon, C. 1977. *Description du livre des figures hiéroglyphiques de Nicolas Flamel.* Montreal: Aurore.

Gässmann, E. 1974. *Antiqui und Moderni im Mittelalter*. Vienna: Shöningh.

Gourevitch, A. 1983. *Les Catégories de la culture médiévale*. Paris: Gallimard.

Goux, J. J. 1978. *Les Iconoclastes*. Paris: Seuil.

Graus, F. 1975. *Lebendige Vergangenheit: Ueberlieferung im Mittelalter und in den Vorstellungen des Mittelalters*. Vienna: Bohlau.

Greimas, A. J. 1976. *Sémiotique et sciences sociales*. Paris: Seuil.

Greimas, A. J., and J. Courtes. 1979. *Sémiotique: Dictionnaire raisonné de la théorie du language*. Paris: Hachette.

Gumbrecht, H. 1977. "Toposforschung, Begriffsgeschichte und Formen der Zeiterfahrung im Mittelalter." In *Beitrage zum romanischen Mittelalter*. Edited by K. Baldinger. Tubingen: Niemeyer. Pp. 1–16.

Haidu, P. 1977. "Repetition: Modern Reflections on Medieval Esthetics." *Modern Language Notes* 92:875–87.

Jauss, H. R. 1970. "Littérature médiévale et théorie des genres." *Poétique* 1:79–101.

———. 1977a. *Alterität und Modernität der mittelalterlichen Literatur*. Munich: W. Fink.

———. 1977b. "Littérature médiévale et expérience esthétique." *Poétique* 31:322–336.

———. 1978. *Pour une esthétique de la réception*. Paris: Gallimard.

———. 1979. "Esthétique de la réception et communication littéraire." Unpublished article.

———. 1981. "Esthétique de la réception et communication littéraire." *Critique* 37:1116–30.

Jimenez, M. 1973. *Adorno: Art, idéologie et théorie de l'art*. Paris: Bourgeois, 10/18.

Kirckpatrick, R. 1978. *Dante's Paradiso and the Limitations of Modern Criticism*. New York: Cambridge University Press.

Köhler, E. 1977. "Gattungsgeschichte un Gesellschaftssystem." *Romanistische Zeitschrift* I:7–22.

Krauss, W. 1959. "Literaturgeschichte als Geschichtlicher Auftrag." In *Studien une Aufsätze*. Berlin: Rütten and Loening.

Lacoue-Labarthe, P., and J. L. Nancy. 1978. *L'Absolu littéraire*. Paris: Seuil.

Leclercq, J., C. H. Talbot, and H. M. Rochais. 1957. *Sancti Bernardi Opera*. Rome.

Legendre, P. 1974. *L'Amour du censeur*. Paris: Seuil.

Le Goff, J. 1977. *Pour un autre moyen âge*. Paris: Gallimard.

———. 1978. "L'Histoire nouvelle." In *La Nouvelle Histoire*. Edited by J. Le Goff, R. Chartier, and J. Revel. Paris: Retz.

———. 1981. *La Naissance du purgatoire*. Paris: Gallimard.

Le Roy Ladurie, E. 1973. *Le Territoire de l'historien*. Paris: Gallimard.

Limentani, A. 1978. "Les Nouvelles Méthodes de la critique et l'étude des chansons de geste." In *Charlemagne et l'épopée romane*. Edited by M. Tyssens and C. Thiry. Paris: Belles Lettres. Pp. 295–334.

Lohner, E. 1978. "The Intrinsic Method." In *The Disciplines of Criticism*. Edited by P. Demetz. New Haven: Yale University Press. Pp. 147–72.

Marin, L. 1973. *Utopiques: Jeux d'espace*. Paris: Minuit.

Marrou, H. I. 1954. *De la connaissance historique*. Paris: Seuil.

Méla, C. 1978. "Pour une esthétique médiévale." *Le Moyen Âge* 84:113–27.

———. 1984. *La Reine et le graal*. Paris: Seuil.

Meschonnic, H. 1978. *Pour la poétique*. Vol. 5. Paris: Gallimard.

Milner, J. C. 1978. *L'Amour de la langue*. Paris: Seuil.

Mittelalterliche Studien: Erich Köhler zum Gedenken. 1984. Edited by H. Krauss and D. Rieger. Heidelberg: Carl Winter.

Moos, P. von. 1974. *Mittelalterliche Forschung ung Ideologiecritik*. Munich: Fink.

Morin, E. 1977. *La Méthode I: La Nature de la nature*. Paris: Seuil.

Moser, W. 1979. "Kant: Origin and Utopia." *Studies in Eighteenth Century Culture* 8:253–68.

Mouralis, B. 1975. *Les Contre-littératures*. Paris: P.U.F.

Ouspenski, B. A. 1976. "Historia sub specie semioticae." In Y. M. Lotman and B. A. Ouspenski, *Travaux sur les systèmes de signes*. Brussels: Complexe. Pp. 141–51.

Panofsky, E. 1957. *Meaning in the Visual Arts*. Garden City: Doubleday Anchor.

Parain-Vial, J. 1966. *La Nature du fait dans les sciences humaines*. Paris: P.U.F.

Patte, D. and A. 1978. *Pour une exégèse structurale*. Paris: Seuil.

Perrone-Moisés, L. 1976. "L'Intertextualité critique." *Poétique* 27:372–84.

Planche, A. 1976. "Moyen Age et presse quotidienne." *Perspectives médiévales* 2:79–84.

Prieto, L. 1971. *Lineamenti di semiologia*. Bari: Laterza.

Reiss, T. 1979. "Archéologie du discours et critique épistémologique." In *Littérature et philosophie*. Edited by P. Garvel. Montreal: Bellarmin; Paris: Desclée.

Rossman, R. 1975. *Perspectives of Irony in Medieval Literature*. Paris and The Hague: Mouton.

Ruprecht, H. G. 1978. "Pour un projet de théorie de la littérature." *Documents de travail*. Centre International de Sémiotique d'Urbino. Nos. 72–73.

Serres, M. 1968. *Hermès I: La Communication*. Paris: Minuit.

———. 1982. *Genèse*. Paris: Grasset.

Stempel, W., and R. Koselleck. 1973. "Geschichte, Ereignis und Erzählung." *Poetik und Hermeneutik* 5.

Stierle, K. 1977. "Identité du discours et transgression lyrique." *Poétique* 32:442–58.

Todorov, T. 1978a. *Les Genres du discours*. Paris: Seuil.

———. 1978b. *Symbolisme et interprétation*. Paris: Seuil.

Valesio, P. 1978. "The Practice of Literary Semiotics." *Documents de travail*. Centre International de Sémiotique d'Urbino. No. 71.

Vance, E. 1979. "Modern Medievalism and the Understanding of Understanding." *New Literary History* 10:377–83.

Veyne, P. 1971. *Comment on écrit l'histoire*. Paris: Seuil.

Warning, R. 1975. *Receptionsaesthetic*. Munich: W. Fink.

White, H. 1973. *Metahistory: The Historical Imagination in Nineteenth-Century Europe*. Baltimore: Johns Hopkins University Press.

Whyte, L. L. 1962. *The Unconscious before Freud*. London: Tavistock.

Zumthor, P. 1972. *Essai de poétique médiévale*. Paris: Seuil.

———. 1975. *Langue, texte, énigme*. Paris: Seuil.

———. 1978. *Le Masque et la lumière: La Poétique des grands rhétoriqueurs*. Paris: Seuil.

———. 1983. *Introduction à la poésie orale*. Paris: Seuil.

———. 1984. *La Poésie et la voix dans la civilisation médiévale*. Paris: P.U.F.